SUBJECTIVE ATLAS OF PALESTINE

SUBJECTIVE ATLAS OF PALESTINE

Edited by Annelys de Vet

010 Publishers, Rotterdam 2007

CONTENTS

7	**A quest for normalcy** *Hassan Khader*
10	**On this earth** *Mahmoud Darwish*
12	**Maps of Palestine**
20	**My Palestine** *Inass Yassin*
22	**Art School drawings after four years in Nablus** *Hafez Omar*
24	**Good morning Palestine** *Hosni Radwan*
26	**This week in Palestine**
28	**Cultural Events april 2007** *This week in Palestine*
35	**A normal day in the Cultural Palace, Ramallah** *Sami Shana'h*
36	**A Palestinian music collection** *Reem Fadda*
40	**Well informed** *Majd Abdel Hamid*
44	**Daily reflections on the news** *Baha Boukhari*
48	**In the absence of a currency** *Shuruq Harb*
52	**Imagining a currency** *Hosni Radwan*
54	**The yellow cabs of Palestine** *Majd Abdel Hamid*
56	**Colour correction** *Yazan Khalili*
58	**Clean Ramallah** *Majd Abdel Hamid & Rudy J. Luijters*
60	**Twelve ways to eat chickpeas** *Suleiman Mansour*
62	**A user's guide to Argeelah** *Munther Jaber*
64	**Selection of Argeelah designs** *Munther Jaber*
66	**Smoke** *Mamoun Shrietch*
68	**What better time than Christmas to discuss the positive sides of life** *Khaled Jarrar*
70	**Children in Gaza trying to play in the world's largest prison** *Shareef Sarhan*
72	**The creations of the Palestinians** *Khaled Jarrar*
74	**Palestinian floor tiles** *Lena Sobeh*
76	**Palestinian dress #1** *Mohanad Yaqubi*

CONTENTS

82 **Palestinian dress #2** *Mohanad Yaqubi*
88 **The flowering heritage of Palestine** *Khalil Sakakini Cultural Centre*
92 **Beautiful Palestine** *Majdi Hadid*
100 **Beautiful Palestine, still under occupation** *Majdi Hadid*
102 **Architectural possibilities for the wall** *Senan Abdelqader Architects (Senan Abdelqader, Inas Moussa)*
104 **Fragmentation of the wall** *Senan Abdelqader Architects (Senan Abdelqader, Inas Moussa)*
106 **The extremities of Ramallah** *Majd Abdel Hamid*
108 **Signs for what's usually prohibited, but not in Palestine** *Sami Shana'ah*
109 **New road signs for Palestine** *Maissoon Sharkawi*
110 **At the checkpoint** *Khaled Jarrar*
112 **Documents that I needed to travel outside Palestine** *Majdi Hadid*
114 **My father's Palestinian nationality** *Baha Boukhari*
116 **My own house where I cannot be** *Baha Boukhari*
118 **59 years of occupation** *Basel Al Maqousi*
120 **Palestinian refugees in the world** *Awatef Rumiyah*
122 **A lifeline to my brother** *Abed Al Jubeh*
128 **Letter from prisoner Mohammed** *Tayseer Barakat*
130 **Letter from prisoner Ahmad** *Tayseer Barakat*
132 **Letter from prisoner Ali** *Tayseer Barakat*
134 **Letter to prisoner Abu Salah** *Tayseer Barakat*
136 **No news from Palestine** *Khaled Hourani*
144 **New flags for Palestine**
152 **Index of contributors**
158 **Credits**
159 **AlQuds** *Wednesday 18 April 2007*

A QUEST FOR NORMALCY

Hassan Khader

Sometime in the 1980s, a Japanese artist interviewed by a Palestinian journalist was quoted as saying: "If you Palestinians don't prevail, then there is something wrong in life". That sentence has been engraved in my memory ever since – but for the wrong reasons. I keep asking myself: what if something really is wrong in life? After all, thinking of the world as a place where rational choices are made, justice is done and dreams are fulfilled is an indication of too much trust in human intelligence. Fortunately, that kind of trust is being constantly contested and deconstructed by art. Such acts give art a highly subversive quality and explain why it doesn't surrender to conventional wisdom. Nevertheless, it can also explain why we humans are always fascinated by and attracted to art: it gives us another way of seeing ourselves and the world.

This is exactly what a *Subjective Atlas of Palestine* is all about. For a Palestinian, Palestine is a profession, a metaphor, and a reality defying categorization. Looking from outside, the checkpoints, the wall, the Orwellian regime of mobility restrictions and the uncertainty of locating Palestine in a non contested map, seem like a nightmare. From inside, the nightmare isn't less obvious. It's there in all possible details. However, among usually recognized manifestations, it has a comic aspect which can't be seen from a distance; like a surrealist dream come true, where things are not exactly what they seem and negotiating one's identity and place is an endless effort of normalization. Looking from inside, the nightmare is like a disease with which one can live, not only as a *fait accompli* but as a tactic of survival. Tactics of survival bring out the best as well as the worst of human behaviour.

The Palestinians are locked somewhere in the middle. Not an easy position for people who strive just to be 'normal' like others. Normalcy is not to be taken for granted, it has to be imagined and invented. Mothers sending their children to school in the morning, lovers meeting in a coffee shop, labourers on their way to work, taxi drivers waiting for passengers, teenagers roaming the streets, middle-aged men smoking water pipes and reading newspapers. All these people know that their reality is fragile and their tranquillity artificial. Yet they make the best of both, as if the world were stable and they are in control.

There is a lot of melancholy hanging in the air, a sense of black humour and even boredom. The map is formed and deformed, joyfully or sarcastically; daily life activities are cherished as precious proofs of resilience. Normalcy can be achieved in different ways, by different means. No-one would stop for a moment to ask: "How can I normalize my life?" The question is: "How can I keep time-tested means of normalcy functioning and oiled?" Palestine as a metaphor is much more complicated and multi-layered than the one portrayed by political rhetoric.

Behind every truth there is a much deeper one. The potential of Palestine as a metaphor has always been rich. The Palestinians are tired, they need a break. The energies they invest just to be like anyone else, their quest for a normal life and the hopes they nourish, are channelled into a tortured relationship with time and place. I think in such a relationship many people in different parts of the world are able to learn something, not only about the intimate and rich existence of the Palestinians, but about human nature as well.

Hassan Khader (writer, literary critic and editor of the literary journal al-Karmel) was born in Gaza and currently lives in Germany

على هذه الأرض
محمود درويش

عَلَى هَذِهِ الأَرْضِ مَا يَسْتَحِقُّ الحَيَاةَ: تَرَدُّدُ إبريلَ، رَائِحَةُ الخبزِ في الفجرِ، آراءُ امرأةٍ في الرِّجَالِ، كِتَابَاتُ أَسْخِيلِيوسَ، أَوَّلُ الحبِّ، عشبٌ عَلَى حجرٍ، أُمَّهَاتٌ تَقِفْنَ عَلَى خيطِ نايٍ، وخوفُ الغُزَاةِ مِنَ الذِّكْرَيَاتِ.

عَلَى هَذِهِ الأَرْضِ مَا يَسْتَحِقُّ الحَيَاةَ: نِهَايَةُ أَيْلُولَ، سَيِّدَةٌ تترُكُ الأَرْبَعِينَ بِكَامِلِ مشمشِهَا، ساعَةُ الشَّمْسِ في السِّجْنِ، غيمٌ يُقَلِّدُ سِرباً مِنَ الكَائِنَاتِ، هُتَافَاتُ شَعْبٍ لِمَنْ يصعَدُونَ إِلَى حتفِهِم بَاسِمِينَ، وخَوْفُ الطُّغَاةِ مِنَ الأَغْنِيَاتِ.

عَلَى هَذِهِ الأَرْضِ مَا يَسْتَحِقُّ الحَيَاةَ: عَلَى هَذِهِ الأَرْضِ سَيِّدَةُ الأَرْضِ، أُمُّ البِدَايَاتِ أُمُّ النِّهَايَاتِ. كَانَتْ تُسَمَّى فِلسطِينَ. صَارَتْ تُسَمَّى فِلسطِين.
سَيِّدَتي: أَسْتَحِقُّ، لِأَنَّكِ سَيِّدَتِي، أَسْتَحِقُّ الحَيَاةَ.

من ديوان "ورد أقل" ١٩٨٦

On This Earth

Mahmoud Darwish

We have on this earth what makes life worth living:
April's hesitation, the aroma of bread at dawn, a woman's
point of view about men, the works of Aeschylus, the
beginning of love, grass on a stone, mothers living on a
flute's sigh and the invaders' fear of memories.

We have on this earth what makes life worth living:
the final days of September, a woman keeping her apricots
ripe after forty, the hour of sunlight in prison, a cloud
reflecting a swarm of creatures, the people's applause for
those who face death with a smile, a tyrant's fear of songs.

We have on this earth what makes life worth living:
on this earth, the Lady of Earth, mother of all beginnings and
ends. She was called Palestine. Her name later became Palestine.
My lady, because you are my lady, I deserve life.

From: FEWER ROSES 1986 (Translated by Munir Akash and Carolyn Forché)

MAPS OF PALESTINE   12

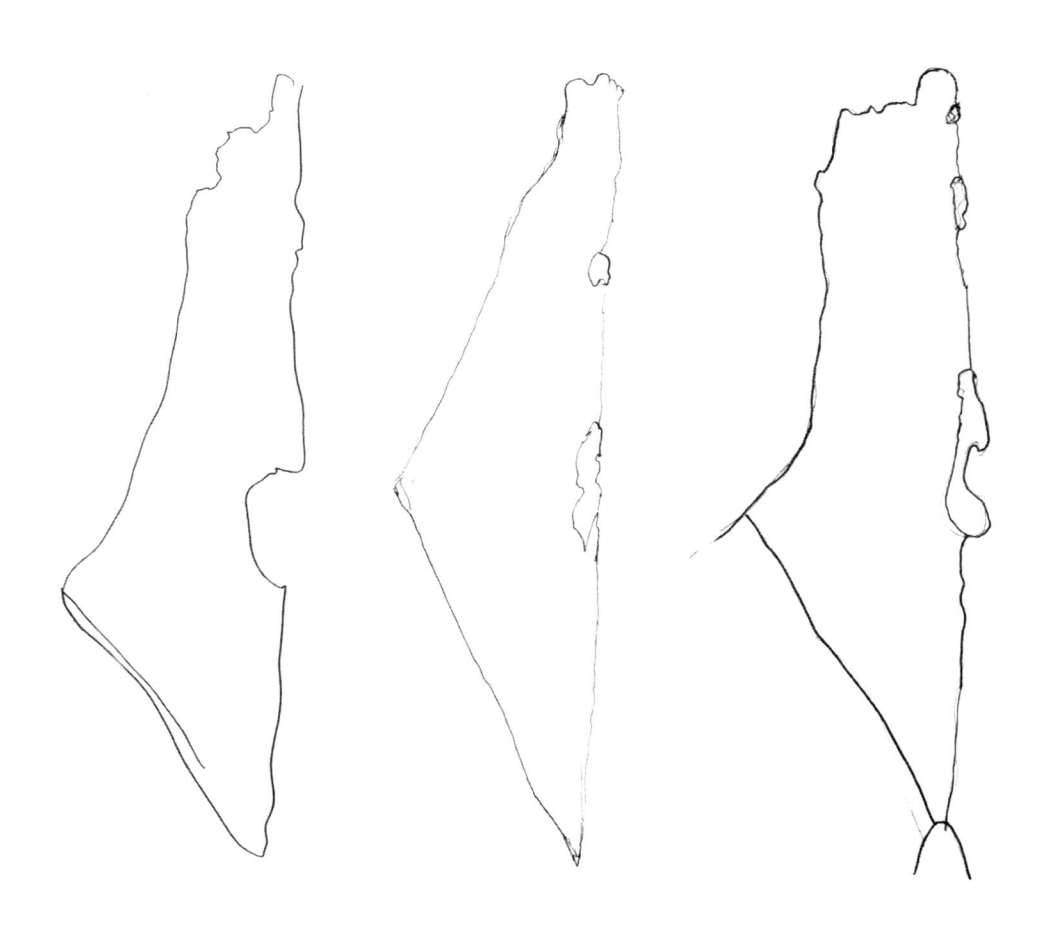

Baha Boukhari   *Mamoun Shrietch*   *Sami Bandak*

MAPS OF PALESTINE 13

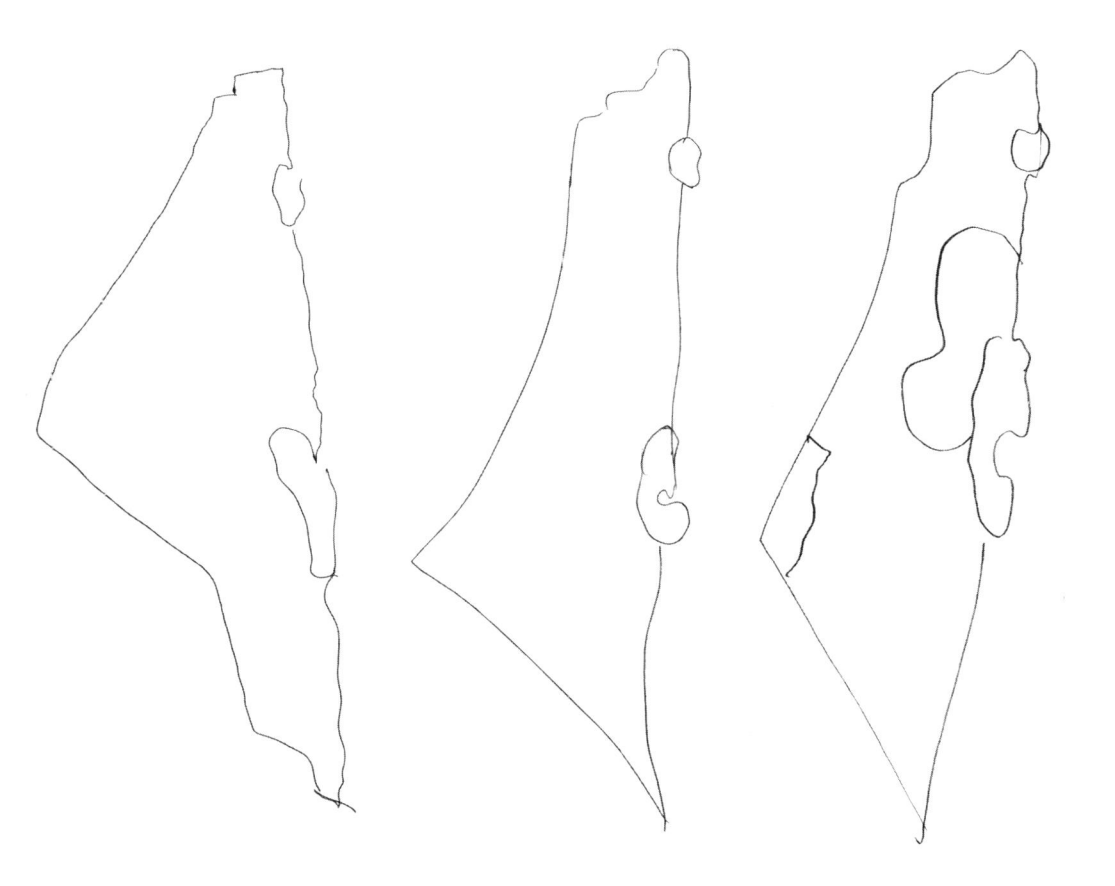

Ahmad Saleem   Mohammed Amous   Khaled Hourani

MAPS OF PALESTINE 14

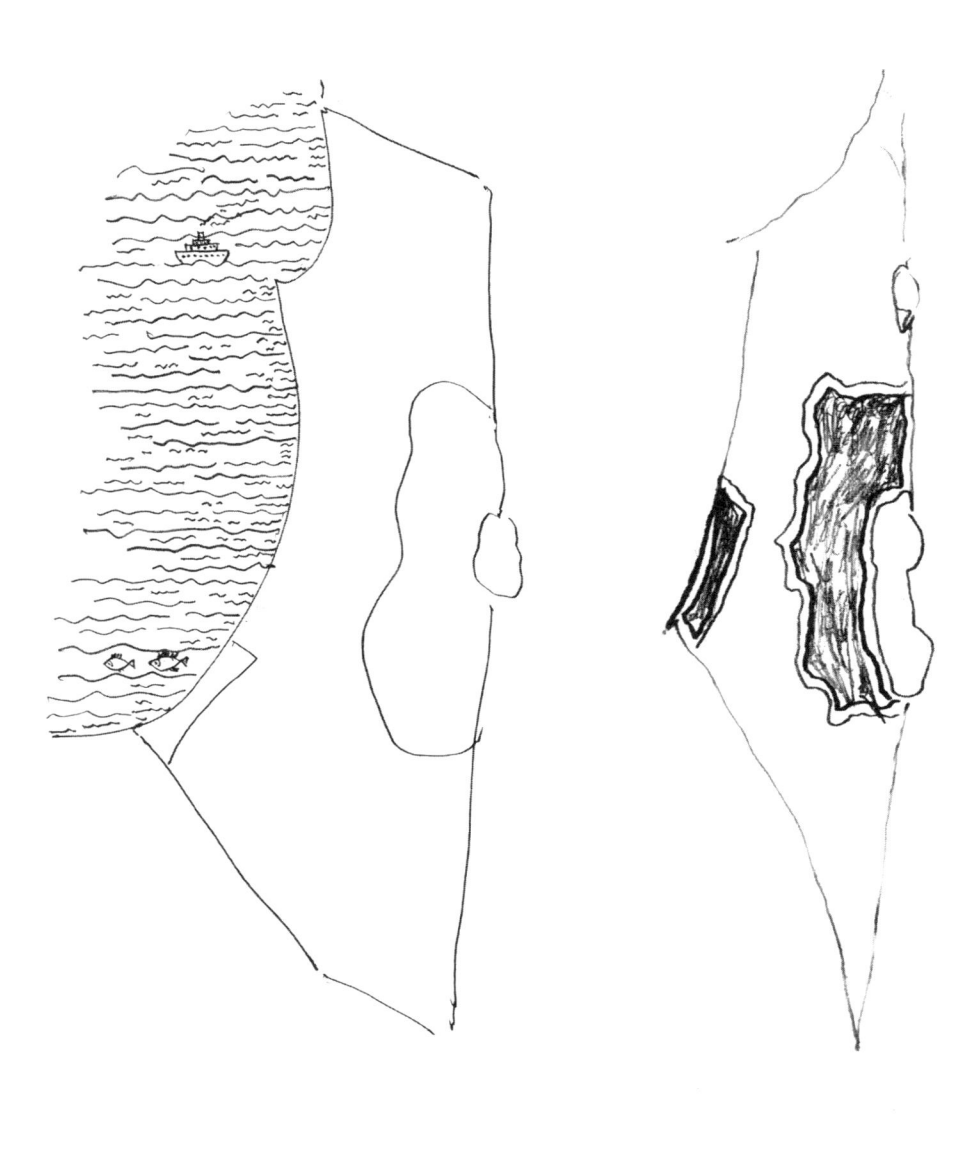

Sameh Abboushi   Tayseer Barakat

MAPS OF PALESTINE   **15**

Munther Jaber   *Reem Fadda*

MAPS OF PALESTINE *Majdi Hadid*   **16**

1948   1967   2003

MAPS OF PALESTINE *Majdi Hadid*   **17**

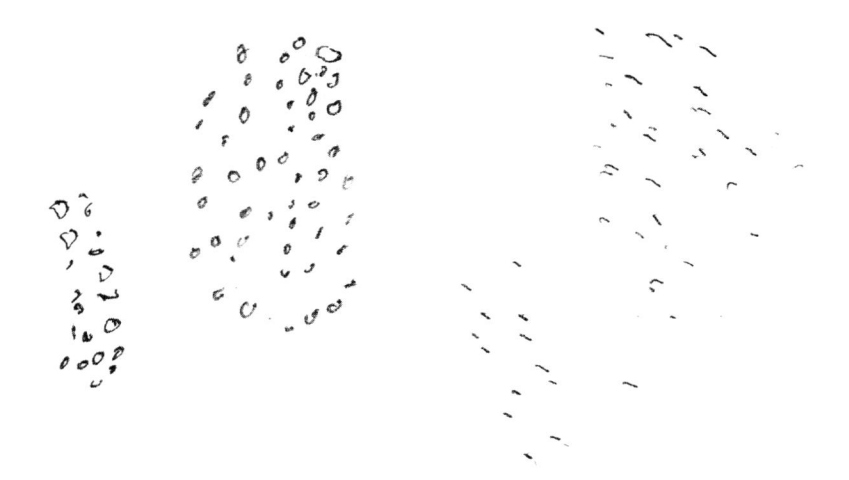

2007   20??

MAPS OF PALESTINE

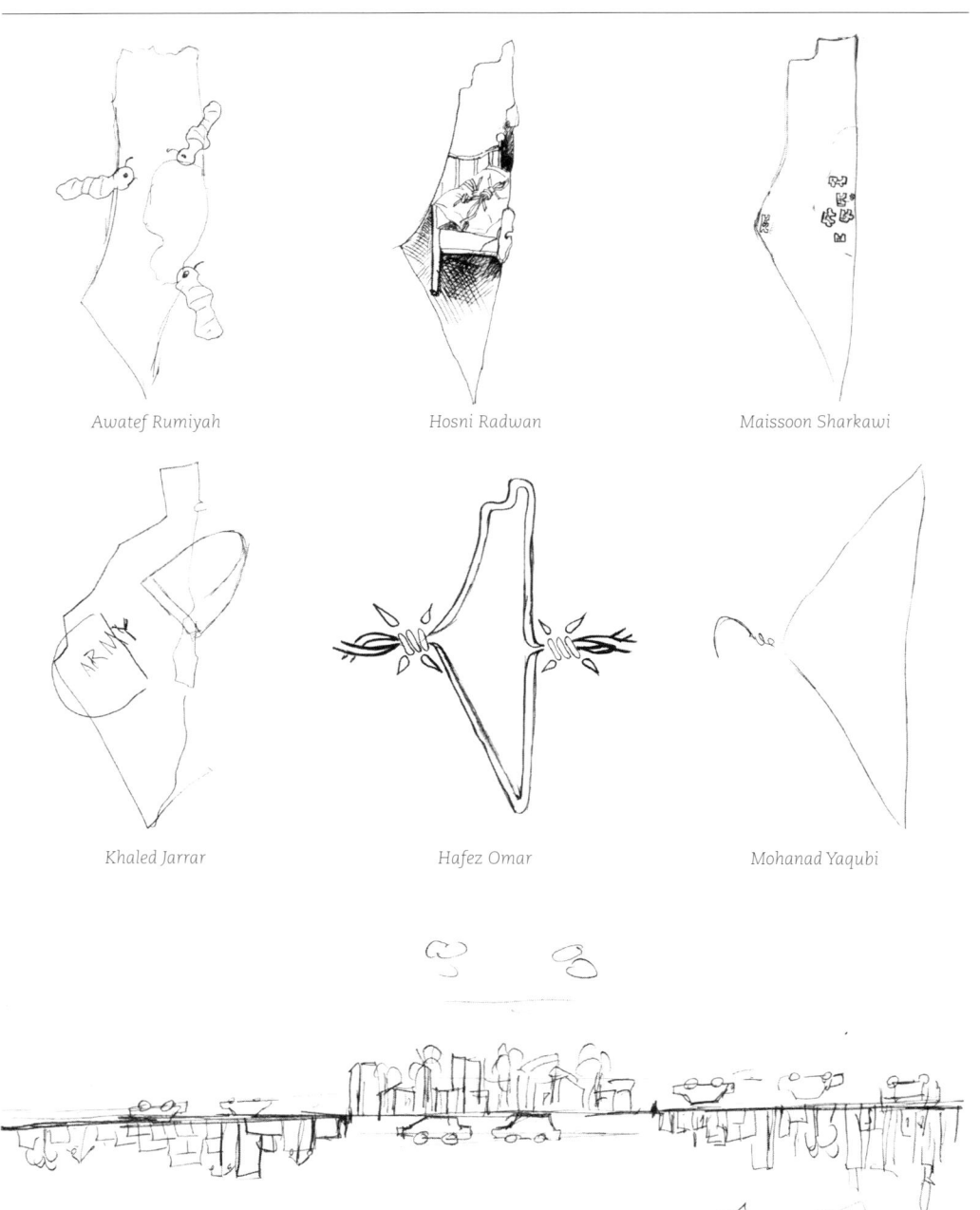

18

Awatef Rumiyah

Hosni Radwan

Maissoon Sharkawi

Khaled Jarrar

Hafez Omar

Mohanad Yaqubi

Inass Yassin

MAPS OF PALESTINE 19

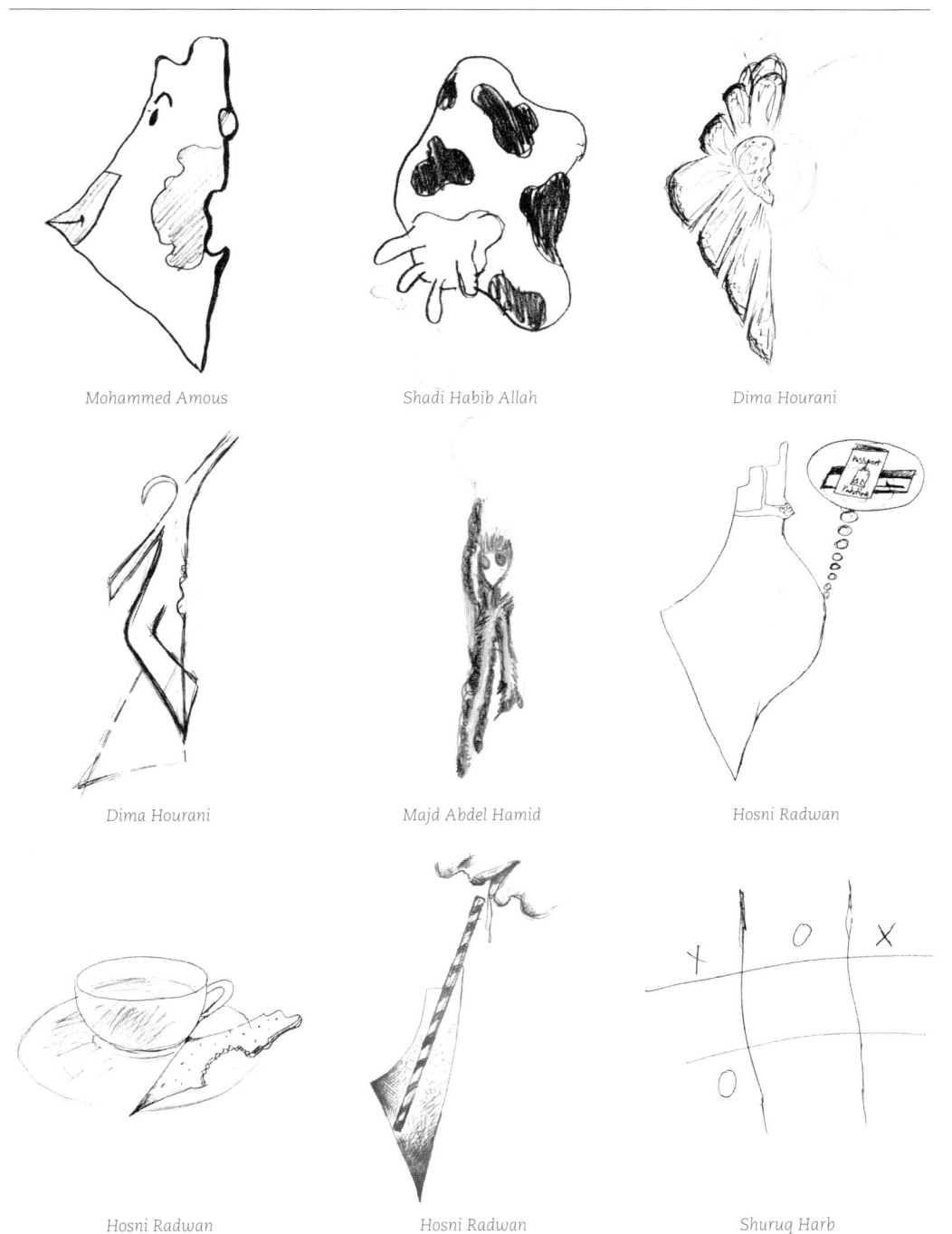

Mohammed Amous

Shadi Habib Allah

Dima Hourani

Dima Hourani

Majd Abdel Hamid

Hosni Radwan

Hosni Radwan

Hosni Radwan

Shuruq Harb

MY PALESTINE *Inass Yassin*

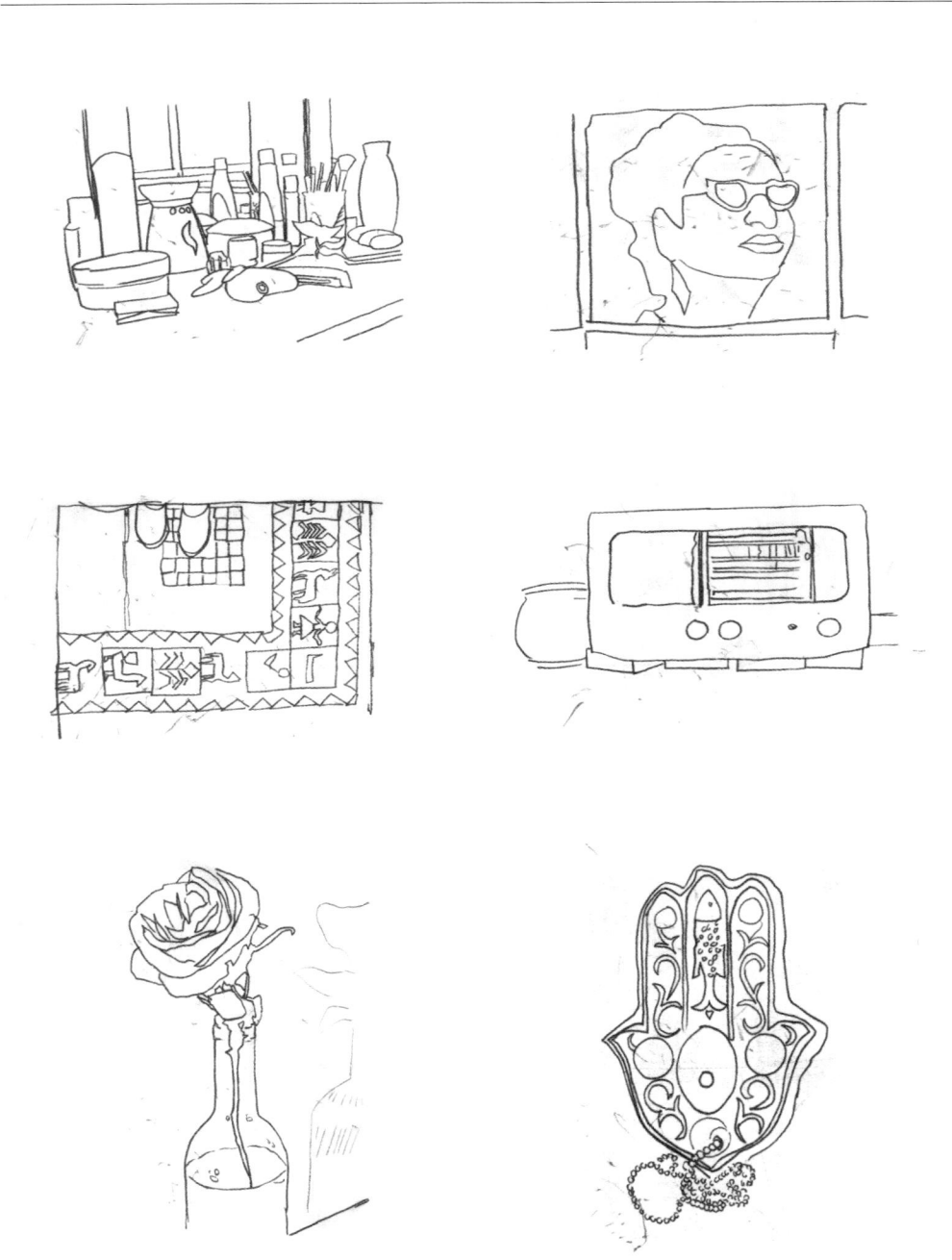

MY PALESTINE *Inass Yassin* 21

ART SCHOOL DRAWINGS AFTER FOUR YEARS IN NABLUS *Hafez Omar*

ART SCHOOL DRAWINGS AFTER FOUR YEARS IN NABLUS *Hafez Omar*

GOOD MORNING PALESTINE *Hosni Radwan* 24

05:28 Liquid balance

06:10 Fresh news

06:55 Lazy step

07:03 The long journey to school

07:05 King of the road

07:08 Presenting a clean Ramallah

07:10 Harvest of the day

07:11 New lemons for a new day

GOOD MORNING PALESTINE *Hosni Radwan* 25

07:12 Bread, bread, bread

07:12 Prose of a stove

07:14 A heavy meal for a light day

07:17 Sizzling falafel

07:26 He sorts them one by one

07:36 Let the sun come in

07:39 Waiting for customers

07:42 The sesame bread is almost gone

THIS WEEK IN PALESTINE   26

Issue No. 41, September 2001

Issue No. 47, March 2002

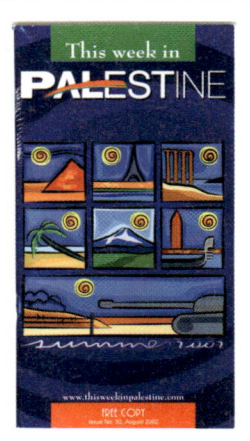

Issue No. 52, August 2002

Issue No. 56, December 2002

Issue No. 61, May 2003

Issue No. 66, October 2003

Issue No. 71, March 2004

Issue No. 72, April 2004

Issue No. 74, June 2004

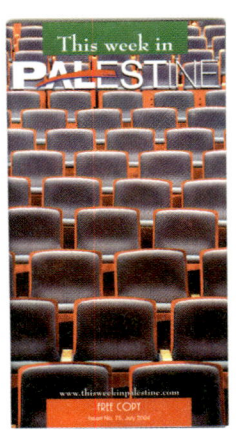

Issue No. 75, July 2004

Issue No. 77, September 2004

Issue No. 80, December 2004

THIS WEEK IN PALESTINE   27

Issue No. 82, February 2005

Issue No. 83, April 2005

Issue No. 88, August 2005

Issue No. 92, December 2005

Issue No. 95, March 2006

Issue No. 98, June 2006

Issue No. 99, July 2006

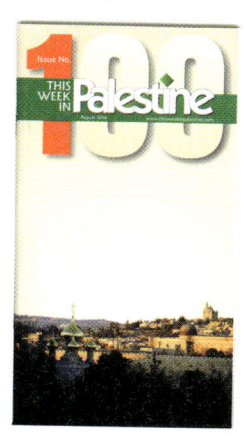

Issue No. 100, August 2006

Issue No. 102, October 2006

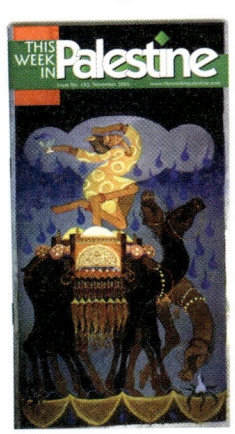

Issue No. 103, November 2006

Issue No. 105, January 2007

Issue No. 107, March 2007

CULTURAL EVENTS APRIL 2007

EAST JERUSALEM

Al-Quds University, tel. 279 0606; Centre for Jerusalem Studies at Al-Quds University, tel. 628 7517; Edward Said National Conservatory of Music, tel. 627 1711; Lutheran Church of the Redeemer, tel. 626 6800; Kenyon Institute, tel. 582 8101; Palestinian National Theatre (PNT), tel. 628 0957; Palestinian Art Court-Al Hoash, tel. 627 3501; St George's Cathedral, tel. 628 1557; Turkish Cultural Center, tel 540 0592

ART
Thursday 5
19:00 **Keep Hope Alive**, dedicated to the Olive Tree Campaign by YMCA & YWCA, curated by Mizuko Yakuwa, *Al Hoash Gallery*

Thursday 12
17:00 **Inauguration** of an exhibition of icons by Bethlehem artist Johnny Andonieh, Russian artist Irine Rafa and other icon writers (through April 23rd, opening hours Monday – Friday 10:00 – 15:00, Saturday 10:00 – 13:00), *St George's Cathedral*

CONCERT
Sunday 1
19:30 Palestine Mozart Festival: **Chamber Masterpieces 2**, *St George's Cathedral*

Tuesday 3
19:00 Palestine Mozart Festival: **Saleem Abboud Ashkar**, *St George's Cathedral*

Tuesday 10
19:00 Palestine Mozart Festival: **Dima Bawab/Andrew Staples**, *St George's Cathedral*

Saturday 14
20:00 Palestine Mozart Festival: **Gala Concert**, *Lutheran Church of the Redeemer*

FILMS
Saturday 7
19:00 **Writers on the Borders**, by Samir Abdallah and José Reynès, *Al Hoash Gallery*

Friday 13
14:30 **Abdülhamit Düserken** (The Fall of Abdulhamit) (Turkish with English subtitles), *Turkish Cultural Center*

17:00 Palestine Mozart Festival: **In Search of Mozart**, documentary, *PNT*

Friday 20
14:30 **Abdülhamit Düserken** (The Fall of Abdulhamit) (Turkish with English subtitles), *Turkish Cultural Center*

Friday 27
14:30 **Abdülhamit Düserken** (The Fall of Abdulhamit) (Turkish with English subtitles), *Turkish Cultural Center*

LECTURES
Tuesday 3
17:00 Palestine Mozart Festival: **Mozart and the Middle East Lecture**, *Kenyon Institute*

Friday 13
15:00 Palestine Mozart Festival: **Edward Said and Music Lecture**, *Kenyon Institute*

Wednesday 18
17:00 **Evening with Jean Vanier** Jean Vanier, founder of L'Arche (international communities for people with intellectual disabilities and their friends) and renowned leader in raising awareness about the suffering of all who are marginalized, will give a talk entitled "Becoming Human: How to Create a More Compassionate Society" (in English), *Ecole Biblique*

PLAYS
Friday 13
20:00 Palestine Mozart Festival: **The Magic Flute**, *PNT*

Monday 16
12:30 Theatre of Oppressed Season: **Don't Lose Heart** - Germany, *Al-Quds University, Abu Dis*

Saturday 21
19:00 Theatre of Oppressed Season: **Demolition** - Spain, *PNT*

TOURS
The tours "Jerusalem, A Palestinian Perspective" are organized by the Centre for Jerusalem Studies of Al-Quds University. The dates of the tours are to be confirmed. For further information please call the Centre for Jerusalem Studies, tel. 02-628 7517

Saturday 7
10:00-13:00 **Easter Rituals in the Old City:** a walking tour to explore "The Church of the Holy Sepulchre", its history, art & architecture (meeting point Centre for Jerusalem Studies), *Centre For Jerusalem Studies*

Monday 9
10:00 **Hills & Valleys in Jerusalem:** the walking tour will start from Lion's Gate towards Kidron Valley, along to Rababah Valley and to Golgotha hill where Jesus Christ was crucified (meeting point Centre for Jerusalem Studies), *Centre For Jerusalem Studies*

CULTURAL EVENTS APRIL 2007 *This week in Palestine* | Issue No. 108, April 2007

Saturday 14
9:00-18:30 *Artas Lettuce Festival:* the tour will start at Solomon's Pools, the group will take a leisurely walk through the beautiful Artas Valley, ending in the village of Artas where they will join performances which include debka troupes and the drama Story of Mona by Ashtar Theatre (meeting point Hind Husseini College), *Village of Artas - Bethlehem*

Saturday 21
10:00-13:00 **Arab Neighborhoods in West Jerusalem:** the tour will take along Mamilla Ma'man Allah (Sanctuary of God), a 13th century Mamluk Cemetery, Katamon, Talbiyeh & Baqa'a where the most striking houses & properties were built and owned by Palestinians (meeting point Hind Husseini College), *Village of Artas - Bethlehem*

MAP OF JERUSALEM

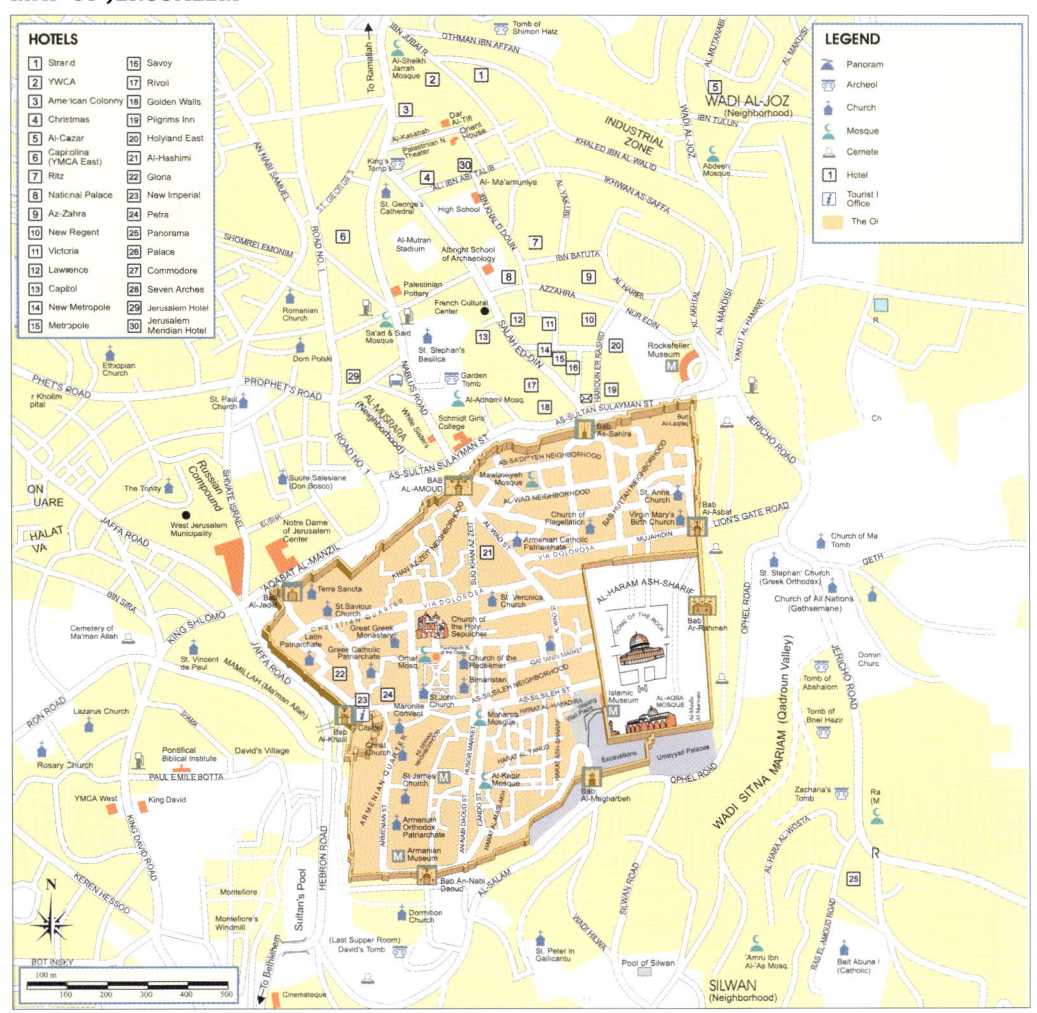

Source: Arab Hotel Association/Pecdar

CULTURAL EVENTS APRIL 2007 *This week in Palestine | Issue No. 108, April 2007*

BETHLEHEM & BEIT JALA

Bethlehem Peace Centre, tel. 276 6677; International Centre of Bethlehem (Dar Annadwa), tel. 277 0047; University of Bethlehem, tel. 274 1241

ART
Sunday 1
10:00-18:00 Inauguration of an exhibition entitled **Troubled Images** organized by the British Council in cooperation with Bethlehem Peace Center, Al Najah University and Birzeit University (through April 8th daily from 10:00 till 18:00), *Bethlehem Peace Center*

CHILDREN'S ACTIVITIES
Wednesday 4
15:00-17:00 **Easter event** with Al Harah Theatre group and bright stars students, *The International Center of Bethlehem*

Friday 6
9:30-13:00 **Friday Club**, *Bethlehem Peace Center*

Friday 13
9:30-13:00 **Friday Club**, *Bethlehem Peace Center*

Friday 20
9:30-13:00 **Friday Club**, *Bethlehem Peace Center*

Friday 27
9:30-13:00 **Friday Club**, *Bethlehem Peace Center*

CONCERT
Monday 9
19:00 Palestine Mozart Festival: **The Magic Flute**, *The International Center of Bethlehem*

Tuesday 10
19:00 **Choir Concert** by the Jerusalem Center for Near Eastern Studies-Brigham Young (Mormon) University in cooperation with Bethlehem Peace Center, *Bethlehem Peace Center*

Thursday 12
19:00 Palestine Mozart Festival: **Gala Concert**, *The International Center of Bethlehem*

Saturday 14
19:00 **German Gospel Choir Musical Night**, musical concert with the German Gospelsterne Choir, *The International Center of Bethlehem*

Monday 16
18:00 **Musical concert by the Spanish pianist Daniel Del Pino**, organized by The Bethlehem Academy of Music, *Bethlehem Peace Center*

Saturday 28
19:00 Musical concert entitled **Mawasem** By Muhsen Subhi and his musical band, *The International Center of Bethlehem*

FILMS
Wednesday 4
19:00 **Passion of Christ**, *The International Center of Bethlehem*

Thursday 5
18:00 **Flushed Away**, *Bethlehem Peace Center*

Thursday 12
18:00 **Garfield 2**, *Bethlehem Peace Center*

Wednesday 18
17:00 Shashat 2nd Women's Film Festival in Palestine, Palestinian Women Filmmakers, films Screening entitled **1000 Women and a Dream** by the director Gabriela Neuhaus & Angelo Scudeletti (with Arabic subtitles) organized by Shashat in cooperation with Bethlehem Peace Center, Ibda'a Center, Dehasheh Refugee Camp, *Bethlehem Peace Center*

Thursday 19
18:00 **Rocky Balboa**, *Bethlehem Peace Center*

Thursday 26
18:00 **The Holiday**, *Bethlehem Peace Center*

Friday 27
19:00 **The Irish Film Making Festival**, *The International Center of Bethlehem*

Monday 30
18:00 **Little Hands** (Arabic with English subtitles) and **The Cane** (Arabic with English subtitles) by the Palestinian Director Abdel-Salam Shehadeh, produced by Ramattan News Agency, organized by The Palestinian Audio Visual Project (PAV)/A.M. Qattan Foundation, in cooperation with Bethlehem Peace Center, *Bethlehem Peace Center*

19:00 **The Irish Film Making Festival**, *The International Center of Bethlehem*

LECTURES
Monday 16
16:00 **Evening with Jean Vanier** Jean Vanier, founder of L'Arche (international communities for people with intellectual disabilities and their friends) and renowned leader in raising awareness about the suffering of all who are marginalized, will give a talk entitled: "Becoming Human: How to Create a More Compassionate Society" (in English and Arabic), *Bethlehem University*

CULTURAL EVENTS APRIL 2007 *This week in Palestine* | Issue No. 108, April 2007

PLAYS

Monday 9
19:00 Palestine Mozart Festival: **The Magic Flute**, *The International Center of Bethlehem*

Saturday 14
12:30 Ashtar's Theatre of Oppressed Season: **Don't Lose Heart** - Germany, *TalitaKoumi School, Beit Jala*

15:30 Ashtar's Theatre of Oppressed Season: **The Story of Mona**, organized by Ashtar Theatre, *Artas Village, Bethlehem*

SPECIAL EVENTS

Wednesday 4
13:30-16:00 **An Open Day for Children On the Occasion of the National Reading Week in Palestine and the Palestinian Child Day**, organized by Tamer Institute for Community Education, in cooperation with Bethlehem Peace Center, Arab Society for Rehabilitation, Directorate of Youth & Sports, Al Khader Center, Beit Jibrin Center, Al Rowwad Center, Directorate of Culture, S.O.S. Ghiras Center at Manger Square, *Bethlehem Peace Center*

Thursday 12
13:30 **Artas Lettuce Festival**, Artas Valleys Opening Speeches, Folklore and Drama Performances

15:30-18:00 **Inauguration of exhibitions**, food and craft stalls, picking fresh lettuce (See www.artasfolklorecenter.net)

Friday 13
9:00 **Hiking from Solomon's Pools to Artas with Palestine Wildlife Society and Artas Folklore Center** with optional traditional lunch
9:30 **Artas Village and Valley Exhibitions**
10:00-15:00 **Children's activities**
15:00-18:00 Beginning of **Drawing Competition and Folklore and Drama Performances**

Saturday 14
9:00 Artas Lettuce Festival, **Hiking from Solomon's Pools to Artas with Palestine Wildlife Society** with optional traditional lunch
9:30 **Artas Spring**, Opening of the Local Market and exhibitions
15:00-18:00 **Artas Valley Folklore and Drama Performances**, Judging of Traditional Drawing Competition

Sunday 15
Artas Lettuce Festival, **Special Hike to Herodium from Artas Village**, with Shat-ha

Monday 16
10:00 On the occasion of the International Health Day, a special program under the slogan of **Investing in Health & Building a Better Future** organized by Bethlehem Peace Center in cooperation with The Medical Relief Society in Bethlehem, *Bethlehem Peace Center*

MAP OF BETHLEHEM

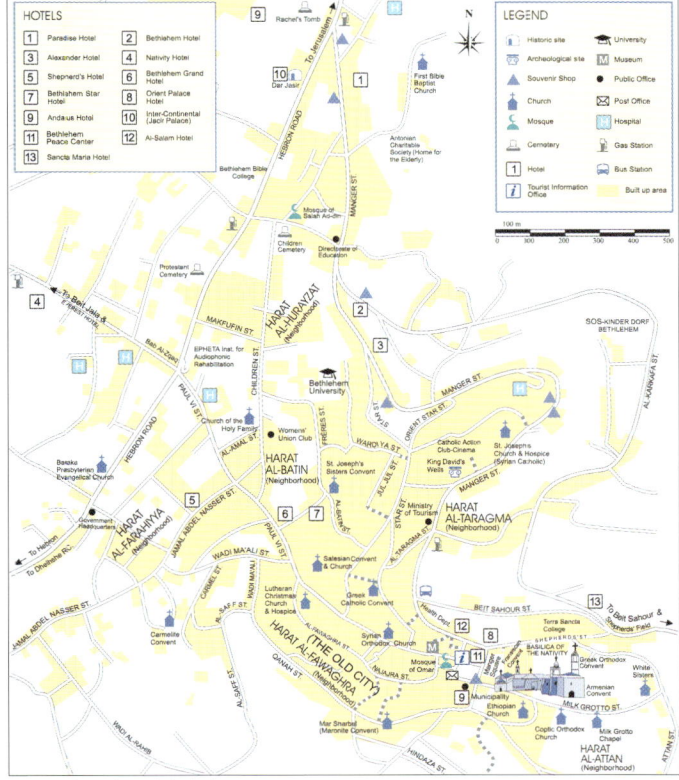

Source: Arab Hotel Association/Pecdar

CULTURAL EVENTS APRIL 2007

HEBRON

Children Happiness Center, tel. 229 9545

PLAYS
Sunday 15
15:30 Theatre of Oppressed Season: **Don't Lose Heart** - Germany, *Children Happiness Centre*

Sunday 22
15:30 Theatre of Oppressed Season: **Demolition** - Spain, *Children Happiness Centre*

Sunday 29
15:30 Theatre of Oppressed Season: **Stories of Seeh Shishaba Village** organized by Ashtar Theatre, *Children Happiness Centre*

JENIN

Khadouri College Tulkarem, Tel: 09-2671073

PLAYS
Monday 23
14:30 Theatre of Oppressed Season: **Demolition** - Spain, *Freedom Theatre, Jenin Refugee Camp*

Wednesday 25
15:00 Theatre of Oppressed Season: **Demolition** - Spain, *Khadouri College, Tulkarem*

NABLUS

Al-Najah University, tel. 2341003; Nablus the Culture Center, tel. 233 2084; Zafer Masri Foundation.

ART
Tuesday 10
10:00-14:00 An exhibition entitled **Troubled Images** organized by the British Council (through April 18th daily from 10:00 till 15:00), *Al Najah University*

CONCERTS
Thursday 5
18:00 Palestine Mozart Festival: **Chamber and Choral Classics**, *Zafer Masri Foundation*

Saturday 14
19:00 **Piano recital** by the pianist Daniel Del, *Al Najah University*

Saturday 28
Oriental Music Evening, *Nablus The Culture*

PLAYS
Tuesday 17
19:00 Theatre of Oppressed Season: **Don't Lose Heart** - Germany, *Zafer Masri Foundation*

Tuesday 24
19:00 Theatre of Oppressed Season: **Demolition**- Spain, *Zafer Masri Foundation*

RAMALLAH

Al-Kasaba Theatre & Cinematheque, tel: 296 5292; A. M. Qattan Foundation, tel. 296 0544; Birzeit Ethnographic and Art Museum, tel. 298 2976; Edward Said National Conservatory of Music, tel. 295 9070; Franco-German Cultural Center, tel. 298 7727; Friends Boys School, tel. 295 6230; Khalil Sakakini Centre, tel. 298 7374; Popular Art Centre, tel: 240 3891; Ramallah Cultural Palace, tel. 298 4704; Sareyyet Ramallah, tel. 295 2706

ART
Wednesday 11
10:00-15:00 A photography exhibition entitled **Seascape** by Jamil Daraghmeh, in cooperation with A.M. Qattan Foundation (through April 17th daily from 10:00 till 15:00, except Fridays and Sundays), *the Ethnographic and Art Museum, Birzeit University*

Saturday 20
10:00-15:00 An exhibition entitled **Troubled Images** organized by the British Council, (through April 28th daily from 10:00 till 15:00 except Fridays & Sundays), *the Ethnographic and Art Museum, Birzeit University*

Monday 23
18:30 **Face to Face**, Photography by German artist Stefan Moses (through April 30th) *Al Sakakini Cultural Center, A.M. Qattan Foundation, Franco-German Cultural Center*

CONCERTS
Sunday 1
17:00 Palestine Mozart Festival: **Chamber Masterpieces 1**, *ESNCM Hall*

Monday 2
19:00 Palestine Mozart Festival: **Saleem Abboud Ashkar**, *Friends Boys School*

Wednesday 4
18:00 Palestine Mozart Festival: **Chamber and Choral Classics**, *Friends Boys School*

Monday 9
19:00 Palestine Mozart Festival: **Dima Bawab/Andrew Staples**, *Friends Boys School*

Wednesday 11
19:00 Palestine Mozart Festival: **Gala Concert**, *Ramallah Cultural Palace*

Thursday 19
19:00 The Spring Concerts Season 2007, **Rafael Serrallet from Spain** – Guitar, organized by the Edward Said National Conservatory of Music, *ESNCM Hall*

CULTURAL EVENTS APRIL 2007 *This week in Palestine* | Issue No. 108, April 2007

Friday 20
19:00 The Spring Concerts Season 2007, **Wasim Odeh accompanied by a group of musicians** – Oud, organized by the Edward Said National Conservatory of Music, ESNCM Hall

Saturday 21
19:00 The Spring Concerts Season 2007, **ESNCM Advanced piano students**, playing with fun and joy – Piano, organized by the Edward Said National Conservatory of Music, ESNCM Hall

Thursday 26
19:00 The Spring Concerts Season 2007, **Issa Murad accompanied by a group of musicians** – Oud, organized by the Edward Said National Conservatory of Music, ESNCM Hall

Friday 27
19:00 The Spring Concerts Season 2007, **Loai Bishara from Palestine 1948 accompanied by a group of musicians** – Oriental Violin, organized by the Edward Said National Conservatory of Music, ESNCM Hall

MAP OF RAMALLAH

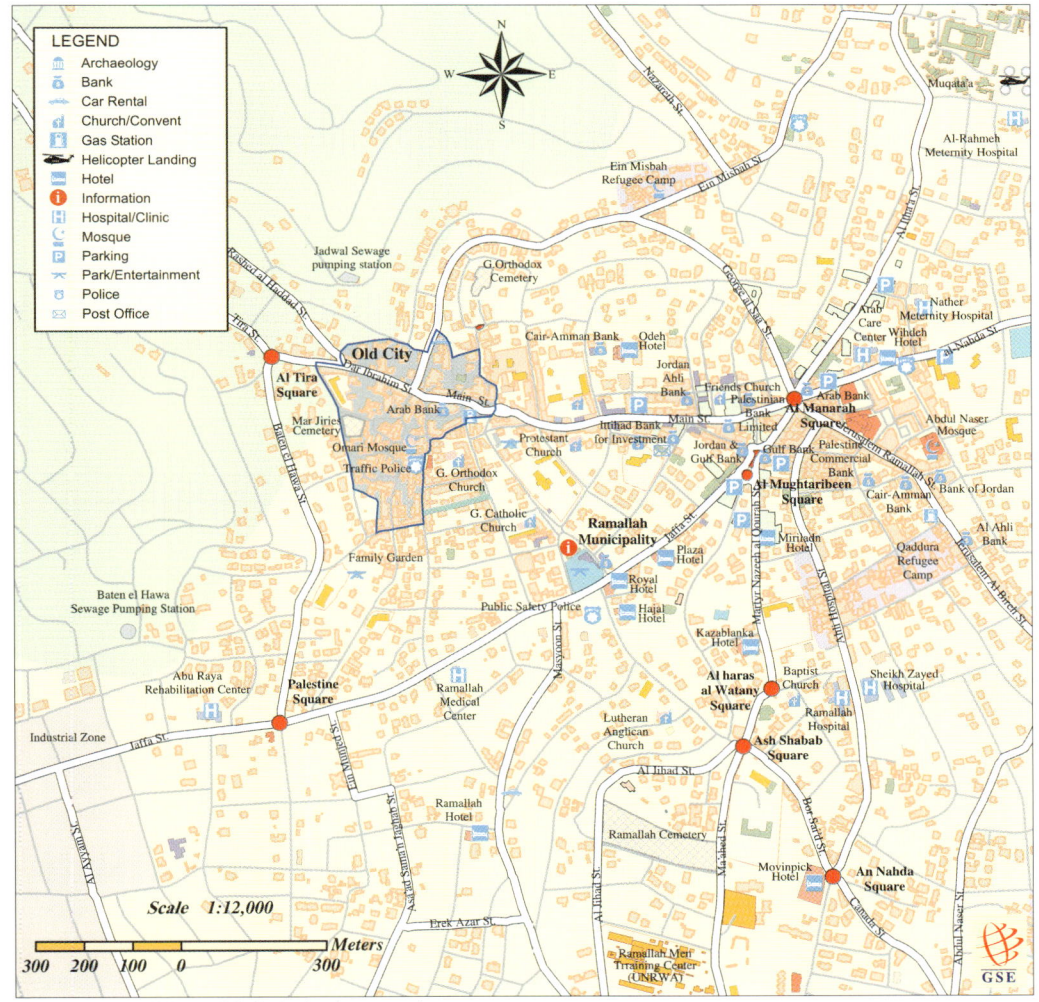

Source designer and publisher: Good Shepherd Engineering & Computing Co.

CULTURAL EVENTS APRIL 2007 *This week in Palestine | Issue No. 108, April 2007*

Saturday 28
19:00 The Spring Concerts Season 2007, **Samer Totah accompanied by Ghofran Group** – Oud, organized by the Edward Said National Conservatory of Music, *ESNCM Hall*

DANCE
Tuesday 24
19:00 **A dance performance by Superintendente de Produção Artística company from Brazil**, Ramallah Contemporary Dance Festival, *Ramallah Cultural Palace*

Wednesday 25
19:00 **Pictures on the Wall**, a dance performance by Okhela company from South Africa, Ramallah Contemporary Dance Festival, *Al Kasaba Theatre & Cinematheque*

19:00 **A dance performance by Ola Qadha from Palestine**, Ramallah Contemporary Dance Festival, *Al Kasaba Theatre & Cinematheque*

Thursday 26
19:00 **Comfort Guidelines & Stringers**, two dance performances by Mancopy Dance Company from Denmark, Ramallah Contemporary Dance Festival, *Al Kasaba Theatre & Cinematheque*

Friday 27
19:00 **Frozen Beliefs**, Homeless Noor excerpt from Hiyaat Noor, Still Moving, Layered Identity, Liquid Renaissance, dance performances by Ya Samar Company from USA, Ramallah Contemporary Dance Festival, *Al Kasaba Theatre & Cinematheque*

19:00 **A dance performance by Amal, Salma and Yezen from Palestine, Ramallah** Contemporary Dance Festival, *Al Kasaba Theatre & Cinematheque*

Saturday 28
19:00 **Hurry Up**, a dance performance by Perpetuum dance company from Serbia, Ramallah Contemporary Dance Festival, *Al Kasaba Theatre & Cinematheque*

Sunday 29
15:00-18:00 **Dance performances by different Palestinian dance groups on the occasion of International Dance Day**, Ramallah Contemporary Dance Festival, *Sareyyet Ramallah*

19:00 **Flatland**, a dance performance by Patricia Porela dance company from Portugal, Ramallah Contemporary Dance Festival, *Al Kasaba Theatre & Cinematheque*

Monday 30
19:00 **24 preludes**, a dance performance by Zappala dance company from Italy, Ramallah Contemporary Dance Festival, *Al Kasaba Theatre & Cinematheque*

FILMS
The Popular Art Centre will screen films from its library for groups of five persons or more by prior reservation only

Tuesday 12
19:00 **Always....Look them in the Eyes**, film by Azza El Hassan, *Al Kasaba Theatre & Cinematheque*

Sunday 15
15:00 **The Little Magic Flute** (Die kleine Zauberflöte, German with English subtitles), *Franco-German Cultural Centre*

Monday 23
19:00 **Festival Ciné-Junior**: Opening of the children's film festival with 'Sherlock Junior', *Al Kasaba Theatre & Cinematheque*

LECTURES
Wednesday 4
16:30 Palestine Mozart Festival: **Mozart and the Middle East** Lecture, *Khalil Sakakini Centre*

LITERATURE
Tuesday 10
18:30 **West Eastern Diwan**, reading with author Adania Shibli and Moritz Zinke, *Franco-German Cultural Centre*

Saturday 21
17:00 **Literary Reading**, reading by German author Esther Dischereit, *Franco German Cultural Centre*

PLAYS
Tuesday 10
19:00 Palestine Mozart Festival: **The Magic Flute**, *Al Kasaba Theatre and Cinematheque*

Thursday 12
19:00 The Theatre of Oppressed Season opening ceremony: **Stories of Seeh Shishaba Village**, organized by Ashtar Theatre, *Ramallah Cultural Palace*

Wednesday 18
12:30 Theatre of Oppressed Season: **Don't Lose Heart** - Germany, *Al Ahliyeh College*

Thursday 19
10:30 Theatre of Oppressed Season: **Stories of Seeh Shishaba Village**, organized by Ashtar Theatre, *Ashtar Theatre*

Thursday 26
19:00 Theatre of Oppressed Season: **Demolition** - Spain, organized by Ashtar Theatre, *Ashtar Theatre*

A NORMAL DAY IN THE CULTURAL PALACE, RAMALLAH *Sami Shana'ah*

A PALESTINIAN MUSIC COLLECTION *Reem Fadda*

Hada Leil
TURAB (Palestinian group)

Basel Zayed: *oud, vocals, composition,* Hisham Abu Jabal: *guitar,*
Yousef Zayed: *buzuq, percussion,* Tareq Rantissi: *percussion,*
Katie Taylor: *string bass,* Mohammed Quttati: *accordion,*
Mohammed Nijem: *clarinet, nay*
Pop

Dal'ouna
DAL'OUNA (French & Palestinian group)

Ramzi Abu Ridwan: *buzuq, vocals, percussion,*
Ramadan Khattab: *nay, vocals, percussion,* Jessie N'guenang:
vocals, flute, Carla Palone: *violin,* Thierry Trebouet: *clarinet*
Folk

Et Nous Aimons La Vie
DAL'OUNA (French & Palestinian group)

Ramzi Abu Ridwan: *buzuq,* Mohamed Amr: *viola,* Yacine Laghrour:
darbouka, Julien Leray: *guitar & vocals,* Thierry Trebouet: *clarinet &
bass clarinet,* Jessie N' guenang: *vocals & flute,* Vanessa Berrue: *vocals,*
Elsa Defosses: *piano & accordion,* Caroline Salmon: *violin*
Folk

Banafsaji
AY WA

Radwan Shalabi: *oud,* Heather Bursheh: *flute, alto flute, vocal,*
Øystein Bru Frantzen: *g-string electric bass, acoustic guitar, vocal*
Jazz

Karloma
KARLOMA

Ahmad Al-Khatib: *oud,* Heather MacDonald: *flute, vocals,*
Rudi Felder: *double bass,* Nasser Salameh: *percussion.* Guest Artists:
Youssef Zayed: *percussion,* Issam Natsheh & Safa' Tameesh: *vocals*
(Produced by the Edward Said National Conservatory of Music)
World

Sada
AHMAD AL-KHATIB

(Produced by the Edward Said National Conservatory of Music)
World

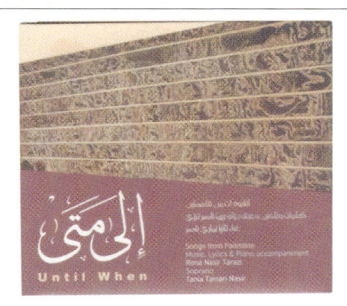

A PALESTINIAN MUSIC COLLECTION *Reem Fadda*

Ila Mata
(Until When)

Music, lyrics & piano: Rima Nasir Tarazi
Soprano: Tania Tamari Nasir
(Produced by the Edward Said National Conservatory of Music)
World

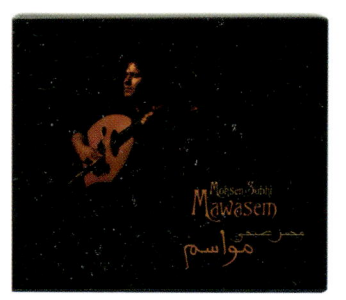

Mawasem
MOHSEN SUBHI

World

Smoke of Volcanoes – Dukhan Al Barakeen
SA3REEN *(a Palestinian group located in Jerusalem)*

Said Murad: composition, Kamilya Jubran: lead vocals, qanoun, Odeh Turjman: contrabass, vocals, Issa Frieij: guitar, Jamal Moghrabi: buzuq, Said Murad: oud, percussion (Produced by Sabreen)
World

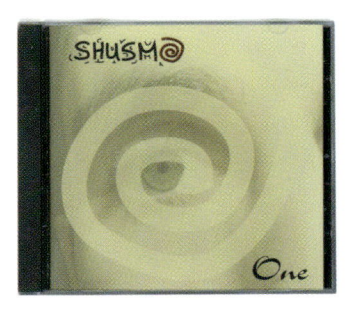

One
SHUSMO *(a jazz band located in NY)*

Tareq Abboushi: buzuq, Hector Morales-Congas: frame drum, Frank Hauch: bass, Thafer Tawil: riq, drubakkeh, cymbals, Lefteris Bournias: clarinet
Folk

Emm el Khilkhal
ORIENTAL MUSIC ENSEMBLE

Suhail Khoury: nai, clarinet, Khaled Jubran: oud, buzuq, Ramzi Bisharat: percussion, Habib Shihadeh: oud, Ibrahim Atari: qanoun, (Produced by the Edward Said National Conservatory of Music)
World

Maawasem il Banafsaj
Seasons of Violet: Love songs from Palestine
RIM BANNA

(Produced in Norway)
World

A PALESTINIAN MUSIC COLLECTION *Reem Fadda* 38

Helm Kbir – The Big Dream
AMMAR HASSAN

(first album of the Arab pop idol/superstar, second runner up, Palestinian singer)
Palestinian Pop Songs

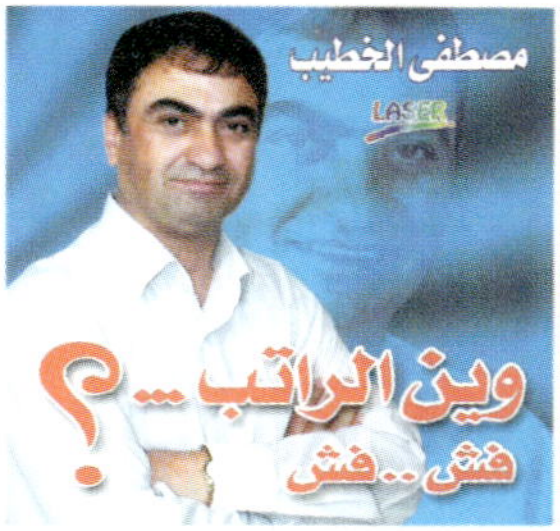

Wein Il Rateb..? Fesh..Fesh
(Where is the Salary..? There is none!)
MUSTAFA AL KHATIB

Palestinian Folklore Pop Songs

Min Sihr il Turath 2006
(The Magic of Folklore 2006)
IBRAHIM SBEIHAT

Folklore Pop Songs

Dabka
AYMAN KABHA

(dabka is a form of Palestinian folkloric dance)
Folklore Pop Songs

Ghinwa Sha'biyah
(Popular Song)
MIX

Palestinian Folklore Pop Songs

Haflet Abu Ajwad Abu Hatem
(Party of Abu Ajwad Abu Hatem)
NASSER AL FARES

Folklore Pop Songs

A PALESTINIAN MUSIC COLLECTION *Reem Fadda*

Afrahuna Al Filistiniyah
(Palestinian Weddings – Part 4)
MIX

Folklore Pop Songs

Zaghareed wa A'rass Min Baladna
(Weddings & Ululations From Our Country)
MIX

Folklore Songs

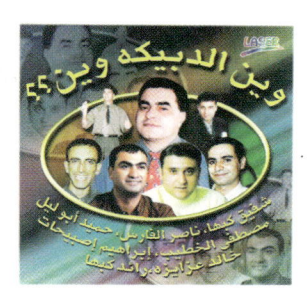

Wein Il Dabeekeh Wein??
(Where are the Dancers of Dabka, Where??)
MIX

Folklore Pop Songs

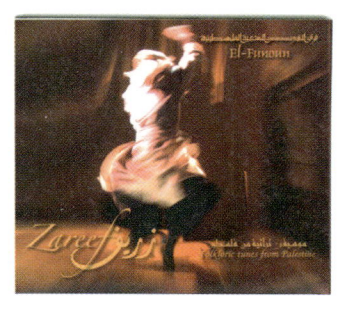

Zareef
EL-FUNOUN

Music by Tareq Nasser, vocals: Sana Mousa, Safa Tamish, Najah Makhoul, Mohammed Musa, Mansour Barghouti & Mohammed Yaqoub
World

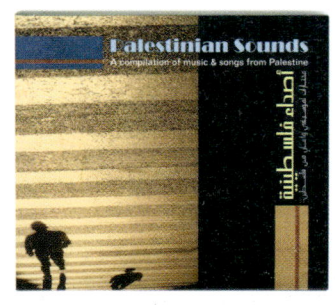

Palestinian Sounds:
A compilation of music & songs from Palestine

El-Funoun, Sabreen, Abado & Co, Oriental Music Ensemble, A'raas, Mustafa Al Kurd, Washem, Odeh Turjman, Al Bara'em, Yoad, Rim Banna, Khaled Jubran & Ahmad Al Khatib, Karloma (Produced by the Edward Said National Conservatory of Music & Yabous Productions)
Folk

Man qala an al Yasser qadd matt
(Who claimed that Yasser has died)
MIX

Political Songs

WELL INFORMED *Majd Abdel Hamid*

WELL INFORMED *Majd Abdel Hamid*

WELL INFORMED

ARTICLE: MAJD ABDEL HAMID / PHOTOGRAPHY: MAJD ABDEL HAMID (LEFT), RUDY J. LUIJTERS (RIGHT)

LIVING INSIDE THE NEWS

Because of the nature of Palestinian life, you are actually living inside the action and every update accounts for a new reality on earth. One of the essential aspects of our lives is keeping up with the news. In the early hours of the morning, most of the people are reading a newspaper.

The rapid change of updates, is also one of the strongest reasons why Palestinian people are intensely attached to all communication tools available. Any new update can affect your daily life; you need to have a clue about what sort of coincidence will take place. In that way the Palestinians are really well informed. They are up to date in terms of news all over the world.

PALESTINIAN NEWSPAPERS:

Al-Ayyam *The Days*
Al Daar *The House*
Al-Hayat Al-Jadeeda *The New Life*
Al Manar (Jerusalem) *The Lighthouse (Jerusalem)*
Al Massar *The Pathway*
Al-Quds *Jerusalem*
Al Sabar (Jaffa) *The Cactus (Jaffa)*
Aml al Ommah (Gaza) *The Hope of the Nation (Gaza)*
As Sbah *The Morning*
As Sennara *The Net*
Assabeel Weekly *The Way Weekly*
Falasteen *Palestine*
Fasl Al Maqal *The Quarter of Articles*
Free Palestine (Gaza) *Free Palestine (Gaza)*
The Jerusalem Times *The Jerusalem Times*
Kul Al Arab *All the Arabs*
Neda al Quds (Jerusalem) *The Call of Jerusalem (Jerusalem)*
Palestine Times *The Palestine Times*
Quds News (Gaza) *Jerusalem News (Gaza)*
Samidoon (Gaza) *Resisting (Gaza)*
Sawt Al Haqq Wal Hurriya *Voice of Truth and Liberty*

SOURCE STATISTICS: 'PALESTINE WEEKLY – JULY 2007'

WELL INFORMED

POPULATION AND DEMOGRAPHY (REVISED 2007)

Palestinian Territory	4,011,078
West Bank (All *governorates*)	2,514,023
Gaza Strip	1,497,055
Jerusalem Governorate	415,573

PROJECTED POPULATION BY AGE (MID 2007)

0 – 17 years	52.2 %
18 – 64 years	44.9 %
65 years and older	2.9 %

EDUCATION (2005/2006)

No. of schools	2,337
No. of school teachers	42,294
No. of school students	1,085,274
No. of school classes	31,963
Students per teacher (*schools*)	25.7
Students per class (*schools*)	34.0
Drop-out rate (*schools 2005/2006*)	0.8 %
Repetition rate (*schools 2005/2006*)	1.5 %
Illiteracy rate for persons 15 years and over (2006)	6.7 %
Illiteracy rate for persons 15-29 years (2006)	0.8 %

CULTURE (2006)

No. of mosques (*in operation*)	1,900
No. of churches	149
No. of newspapers (*in operation*)	12
No. of museums (*in operation*)	5
No. of cultural centres (*in operation*)	86

INFORMATION & COMMUNICATION (2006)

Availability of TV sets	95.3 %
Availability of satellite dishes for households with a TV set	80.4 %
Availability of computers at home	32.9 %
Availability of Internet at home	15.9 %
People (10 years and over) who have access to Internet	18.4 %
People (10 years and over) using a computer	50.9 %
Percentage of households who have a mobile	81.0 %
Percentage of households who have a phone	50.8 %
Percentage of households who view Palestine TV	29.9 %

DAILY REFLECTIONS ON THE NEWS *Baha Boukhari*

Audience for the story

Arab and supports

Smile

No salaries since international boycott

Salary

Waiting

The wall puzzle

Wall Street

DAILY REFLECTIONS ON THE NEWS *Baha Boukhari*

Lebanon and assassinations

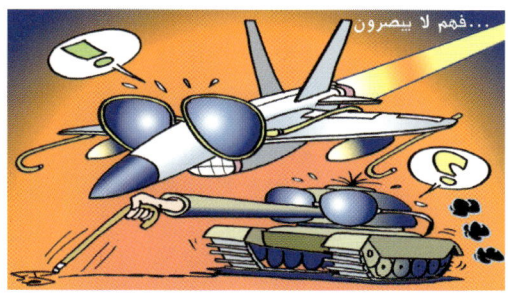

Lebanon and blindness

Lebanon and dove

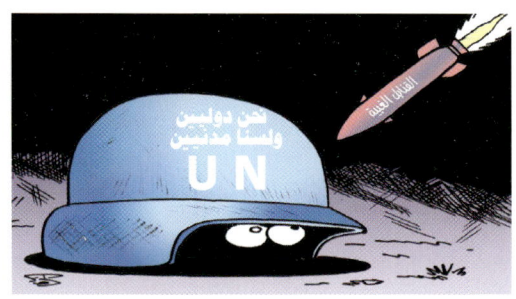

Lebanon and civilian

Olmert and efforts

Lebanon and ceasefire

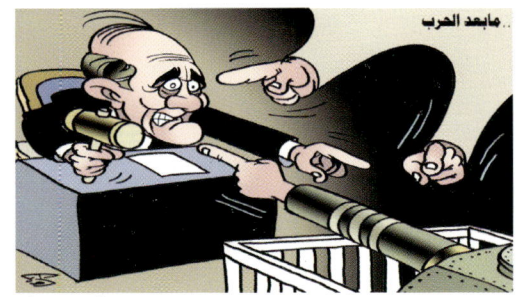

Olmert after war

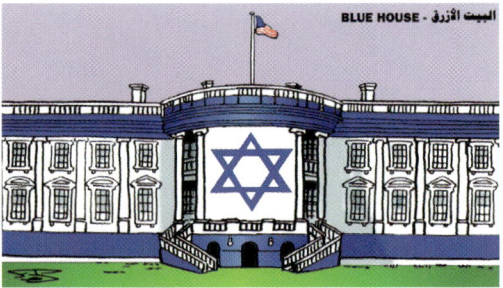

The Blue House

DAILY REFLECTIONS ON THE NEWS *Baha Boukhari*

America and faults

U.S.A. and Condoleezza

Third anniversary of Iraq

The three lights of America

Iraq and Blair

They learn democracy the British way

Liberty and Guantanamo

Saddam and court

DAILY REFLECTIONS ON THE NEWS *Baha Boukhari*

Bush and old strategies

Bush and new strategies

Bush and balance

Bush visits Afghanistan

Kofi Annan and Ban Ki Moon

The new Pope: "Peace for everyone"

Arab wonder

An Arabic endeavour

IN THE ABSENCE OF A CURRENCY *Shuruq Harb* 48

Public Relations Officer, Ministry of Culture
Salary in Israeli Shekels

Director General, Ministry of Culture
Salary in Israeli Shekels

Lab Technician, Medicar Lab
Salary in Jordanian Dinars

Police Officer, Palestinian Authority
Salary in Israeli Shekels

Correspondent, Al-Jazeera & Freelance Producer Assistent
Salary in US Dollars and paid in Euros for freelance work

Supervising copy-editor, Palestinian Times
Salary in US Dollars

IN THE ABSENCE OF A CURRENCY *Shuruq Harb*

Birzeit University Student
Allowance in Israeli Shekels

Birzeit University Professor
Salary in Jordanian Dinars

Public School Teacher
Salary in Israeli Shekels

**Academic Officer,
International Academy of Art Palestine**
Salary in US Dollars

Waiter at Stones Restaurant
Salary in Israeli Shekels

Vender, Al-Arabi Market
Income in Israeli Shekels

IN THE ABSENCE OF A CURRENCY *Shuruq Harb* 50

IN THE ABSENCE OF A CURRENCY *Shuruq Harb*

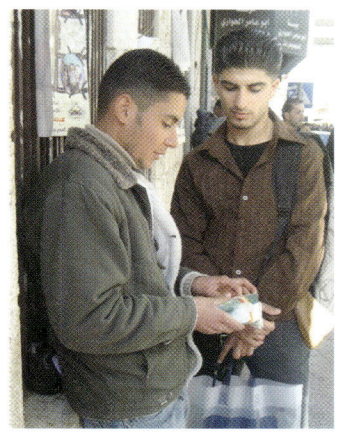

IMAGINING A CURRENCY *Hosni Radwan*

IMAGINING A CURRENCY Hosni Radwan

53

THE YELLOW CABS OF PALESTINE *Majd Abdel Hamid*

Hebron

Bethlehem

Jericho

Jenin

Nablus

Ramallah

THE YELLOW CABS OF PALESTINE *Majd Abdel Hamid*

Al Sa'ah square, Ramallah

Main street, Ramallah

Jerusalem Ramallah Street, Ramallah

Nablus Street, Ramallah

Main Street, Ramallah

Central bus station 'il Mojama', Ramallah

COLOUR CORRECTION *Yazan Khalili*

COLOUR CORRECTION *Yazan Khalili*

CLEAN RAMALLAH *Majd Abdel Hamid & Rudy J. Luijters* 58

CLEAN RAMALLAH *Majd Abdel Hamid & Rudy J. Luijters*

TWELVE WAYS TO EAT CHICKPEAS *Suleiman Mansour*

Hamleh Malan
Green chickpeas

Hamleh Mashwyieh
Grilled green chickpeas with salted water and hot black pepper

Balilah
Boiled chickpeas topped with salt and cumin

Kdameh Safra
Saturated chickpeas and then roasted

Kdameh Beida
Saturated chickpeas with salted water and then roasted

Kdameh Hamra
Saturated chickpeas with spices and then roasted

TWELVE WAYS TO EAT CHICKPEAS *Suleiman Mansour*   61

Kdameh Mlabbas
Saturated and grilled chickpeas, topped with coloured sugar

Mussabaha
boiled chickpeas with tahieneh, lemon, garlic, cumin and salt

Hommus Midammas
mashed boiled chickpeas with garlic, lemon and tahieneh

Fatteh
dry bread saturated in chickpeas water mixed with whole boiled chickpeas and some hommus midammas and lemon

Na'umeh
grounded kdameh safra mixed with boiled wheat and topped with grounded sugar and kdameh mlabbas

Falafel
mashed boiled chickpeas with parsley, garlic, cumin and then shaped like a small ball and grilled in hot oil

A USER'S GUIDE TO ARGEELAH* *Munther Jaber*

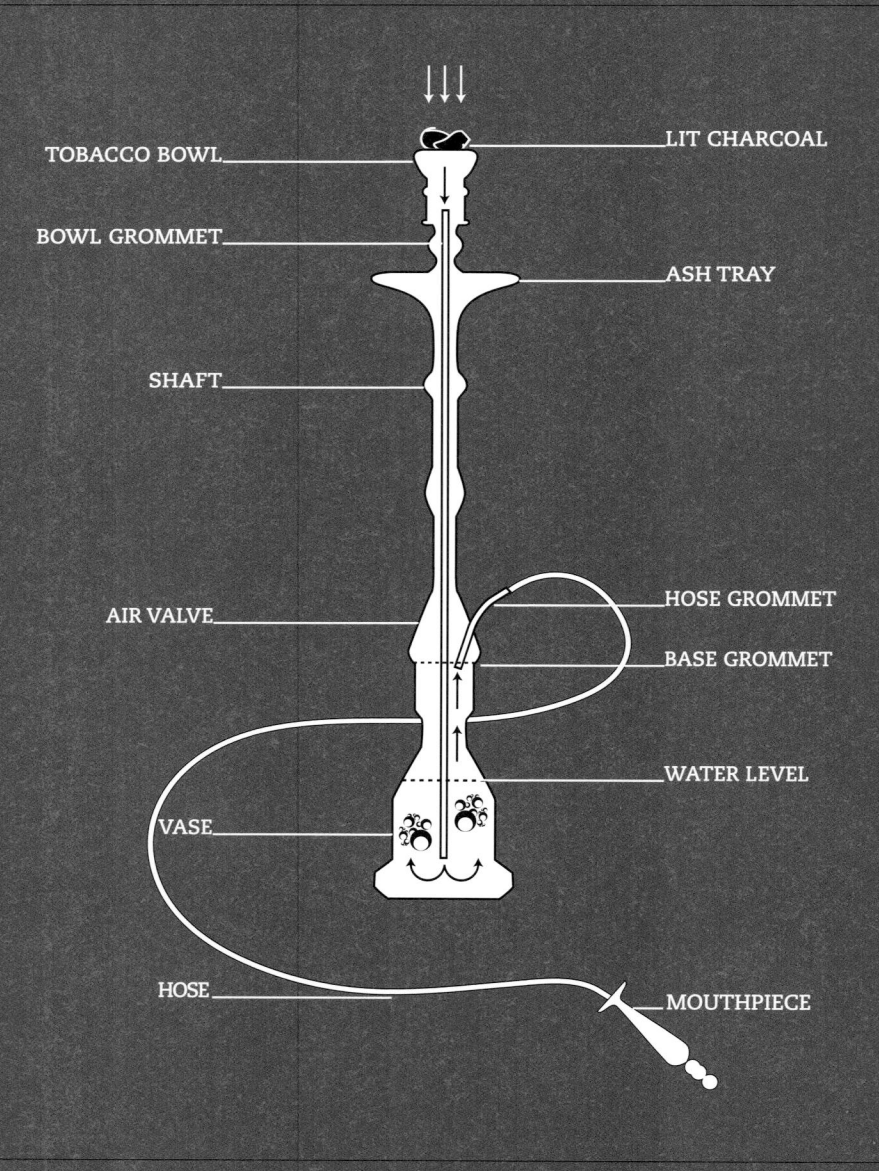

- TOBACCO BOWL
- LIT CHARCOAL
- BOWL GROMMET
- ASH TRAY
- SHAFT
- AIR VALVE
- HOSE GROMMET
- BASE GROMMET
- WATER LEVEL
- VASE
- HOSE
- MOUTHPIECE

FLAVOURS:

- APPLE
- TWO APPLES
- BANANA
- COCKTAIL
- FAKHFAKHENA
- GRAPE
- LEMON
- LICORICE
- MASREY
- MELON
- MINT
- ORANGE
- PEACH
- ROSE
- SUGAR CANDY
- STRAWBERRY
- WATER MELON

A USER'S GUIDE TO ARGEELAH* *Munther Jaber*

1. Pack tobacco lightly in clay bowl

2. Place a piece of aluminium foil tightly over and around the clay bowl

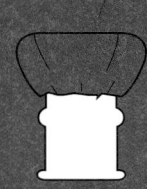

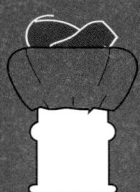

3. Using a toothpick lightly puncture the foil

4. Place well lit charcoal over the foil

---

* Depending on locality, hookahs are known variously as a **water pipe, nargeela / nargile / narghile / nargileh, argeela / arghileh, shisha / sheesha, okka, kalyan,** or **ghelyoon** or **ghalyan**. Many of these names are of Arab, Indian, Turkish, Uzbek, or Persian origin.

Narghile is from the Persian word *nārgil* or 'coconut', and in Sanskrit *nārikela* since the original nargile came from India and was made out of coconut shells. **Shisha** is from the Persian word *shishe*, literally translated as 'glass' (and not bottle). **Hashish** is an Arabic word for grass, which may have been another way of saying tobacco. Another source states: "In early Arabic texts, the term hashish referred not only to cannabis resin but also to the dried leaves or flower heads and sweetmeats made with them". **Hookah** itself may stem from Arabic *uqqa*, meaning small box, pot, or jar. Both names refer to the original methods of constructing the smoke / water chamber part of the hookah. **Narghile** is the name most commonly used in Turkey, Lebanon, Syria, Iraq, Jordan, Greece, Cyprus, Albania, Palestine, Israel and Romania, though the initial 'n' is often dropped in Arabic. *Shisha* is more commonly seen in Egypt, Morocco, Tunisia, Saudi Arabia and Somalia. In Iran it is called **ghalyoun** or **ghalyan** and in Pakistan and India it is referred to as *huqqa*. The archaic form of this latter name, *hookah* is most commonly used in English for historical reasons, as it was in India that large numbers of English-speakers first sampled the effects of the water pipe.

SELECTION OF ARGEELAH DESIGNS *Munther Jaber*   64

SELECTION OF ARGEELAH DESIGNS *Munther Jaber*

SMOKE *Mamoun Shrietch* 66

Tobacco

Tobacco

Tobacco bowl

Water pipe storage

Preparing the bowl

Testing

SMOKE *Mamoun Shrietch* 67

Burning coal

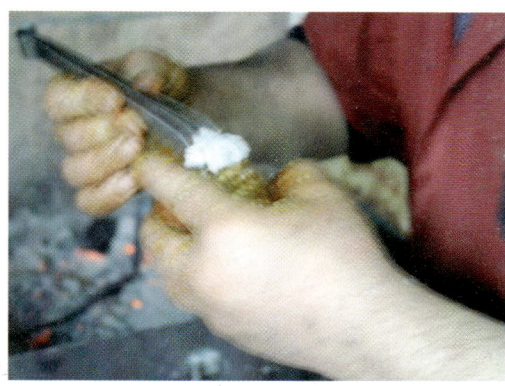

Putting coal on burner

Top of water pipe

Smoking

Smoking

Smoking

WHAT BETTER TIME THAN CHRISTMAS TO DISCUSS THE POSITIVE SIDES OF LIFE 68

Father

Policeman

I am here too

Tired

Sleeping baby

I like Christmas

European

Palestinian

Journalist

Palestinian

From Britain and Scotland

Europeans

European

We catch you

Italian

Khaled Jarrar, Bethlehem 25th December 2006

Christian	Palestinian
Palestinian	Palestinian
Musician	Hat seller
Palestinian	Policeman
Live in peace	Moslim
He's taking photos of us	Merry Christmas
Arabic coffee	Priest
Baba	Indian

CHILDREN IN GAZA TRYING TO PLAY IN THE WORLD'S LARGEST PRISON *Shareef Sarhan*

CHILDREN IN GAZA TRYING TO PLAY IN THE WORLD'S LARGEST PRISON *Shareef Sarhan*

THE CREATIONS OF THE PALESTINIANS *Khaled Jarrar*

THE CREATIONS OF THE PALESTINIANS *Khaled Jarrar*

PALESTINIAN FLOOR TILES *Lena Sobeh / RIWAQ*

PALESTINIAN FLOOR TILES *Lena Sobeh / RIWAQ*

PALESTINIAN DRESS #1 *Mohanad Yaqubi*

PALESTINIAN DRESS #1 *Mohanad Yaqubi*

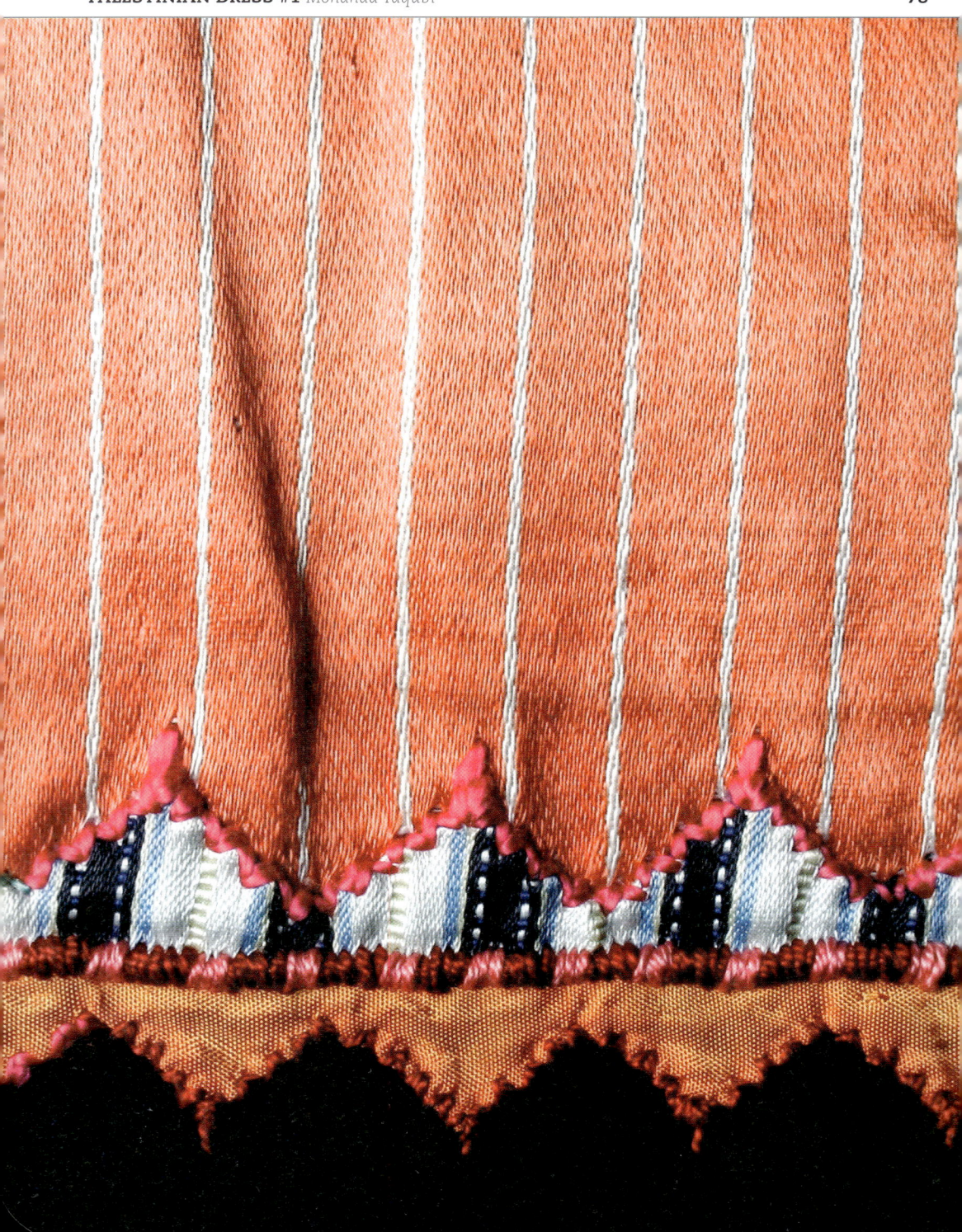

PALESTINIAN DRESS #1 *Mohanad Yaqubi*

PALESTINIAN DRESS #1 *Mohanad Yaqubi*

PALESTINIAN DRESS #1 *Mohanad Yaqubi*

PALESTINIAN DRESS #1 *Mohanad Yaqubi*

PALESTINIAN DRESS #2 *Mohanad Yaqubi*

PALESTINIAN DRESS #2 *Mohanad Yaqubi*

PALESTINIAN DRESS #2 *Mohanad Yaqubi* 84

PALESTINIAN DRESS #2 *Mohanad Yaqubi*

85

PALESTINIAN DRESS #2 *Mohanad Yaqubi* 86

PALESTINIAN DRESS #2 *Mohanad Yaqubi*　　　　　　　　　　　　　　　　　　　　87

THE FLOWERING HERITAGE OF PALESTINE *Khalil Sakakini Cultural Centre* 88

Common Cyclamen *Cyclamen persium*

Crown Anemone *Anemone coronaria*

Red Mountain Tulip *Tulipa agnensis*

Palestinian Arum *Arum palestinum*

Wild Leek *Allium ampeloprasum*

Rock Rose *Cistus icanus*

THE FLOWERING HERITAGE OF PALESTINE *Khalil Sakakini Cultural Centre* 89

Three Thistles *Centaurea hyalolepis*

Common Caper *Capparis spinosa*

Yellow Plume Thistle *Picnomon acarma*

Clammy Inula *Inula viscosa*

Squirting Cucumber *Ecballium elaterium*

White Winter Crocus *Crocus hyemalis*

THE FLOWERING HERITAGE OF PALESTINE Khalil Sakakini Cultural Centre

Fiar's Cowl *Arisarum vulgare*

Pyramidal Orchid *Anacamptis pyramidalis*

Crown Anemone *Ranunculus asiaticus*

Afternoon Iris *Gynandriris sisynchium*

Field Gladiolus *Gladiolus italicus*

Blue Pimpernel *Anagallis arvensis*

THE FLOWERING HERITAGE OF PALESTINE *Khalil Sakakini Cultural Centre* 91

Bristly Hollyhock *Alcea setosa*

Palestinian Pistachio *Pistacia palestina*

Sea Squill *Urginea maritima*

Winter Daffodil *Stenbergia lutea*

Steven's Meadow-saffron *Colchium stevenii*

Narcissus *Narcissus tazetta*

BEAUTIFUL PALESTINE

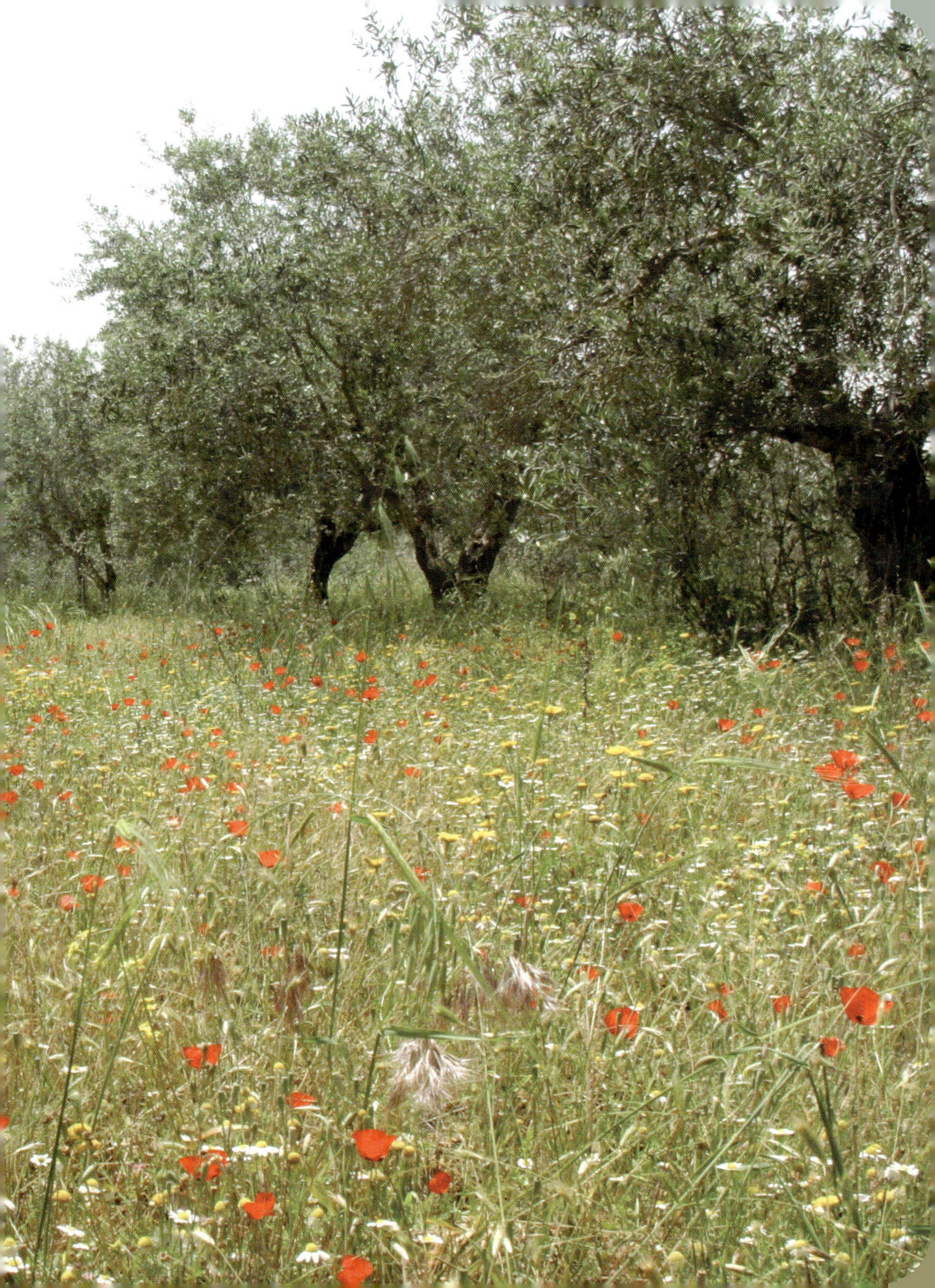

BEAUTIFUL PALESTINE *Majdi Hadid*

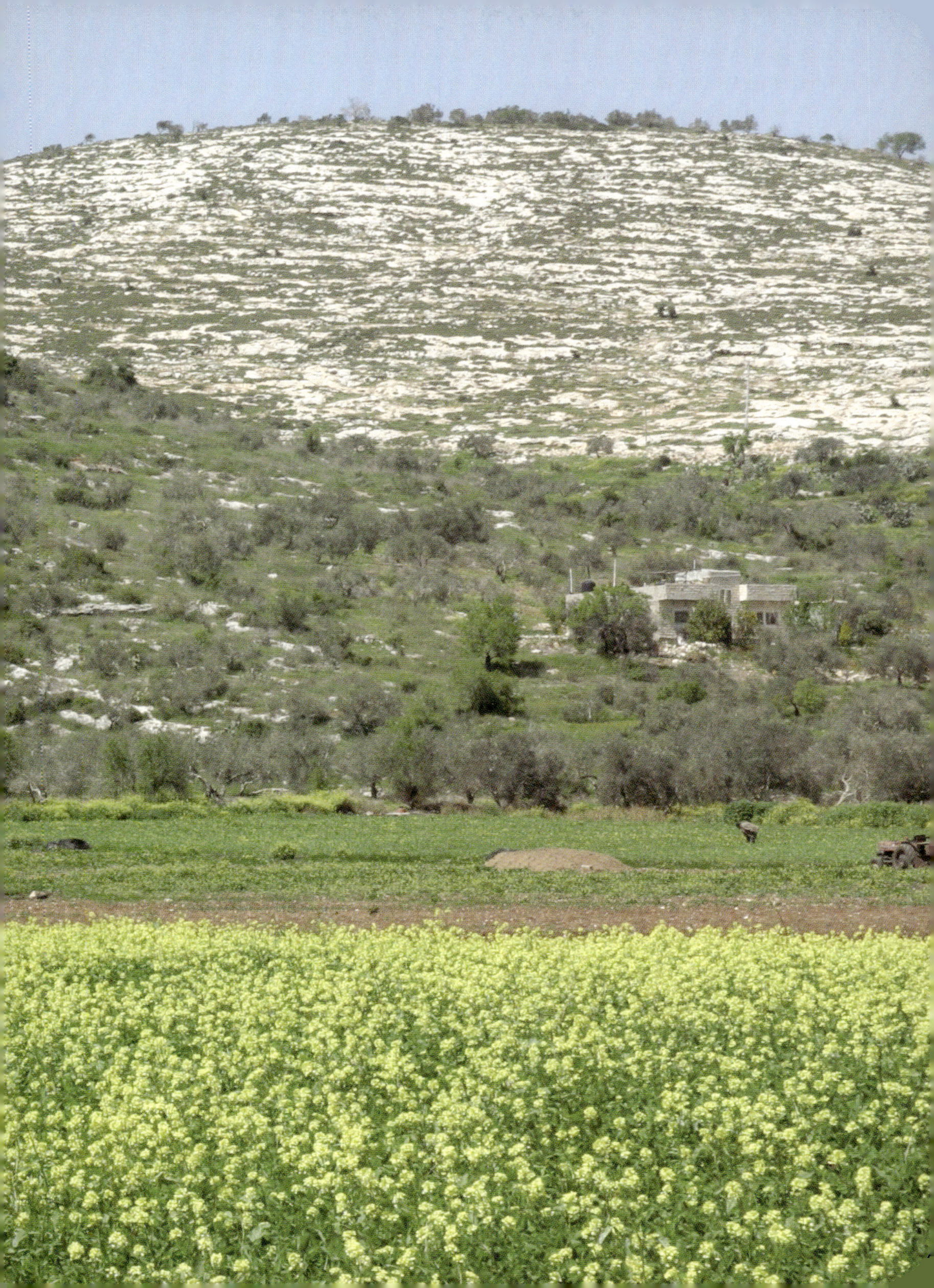

BEAUTIFUL PALESTINE *Majdi Hadid*

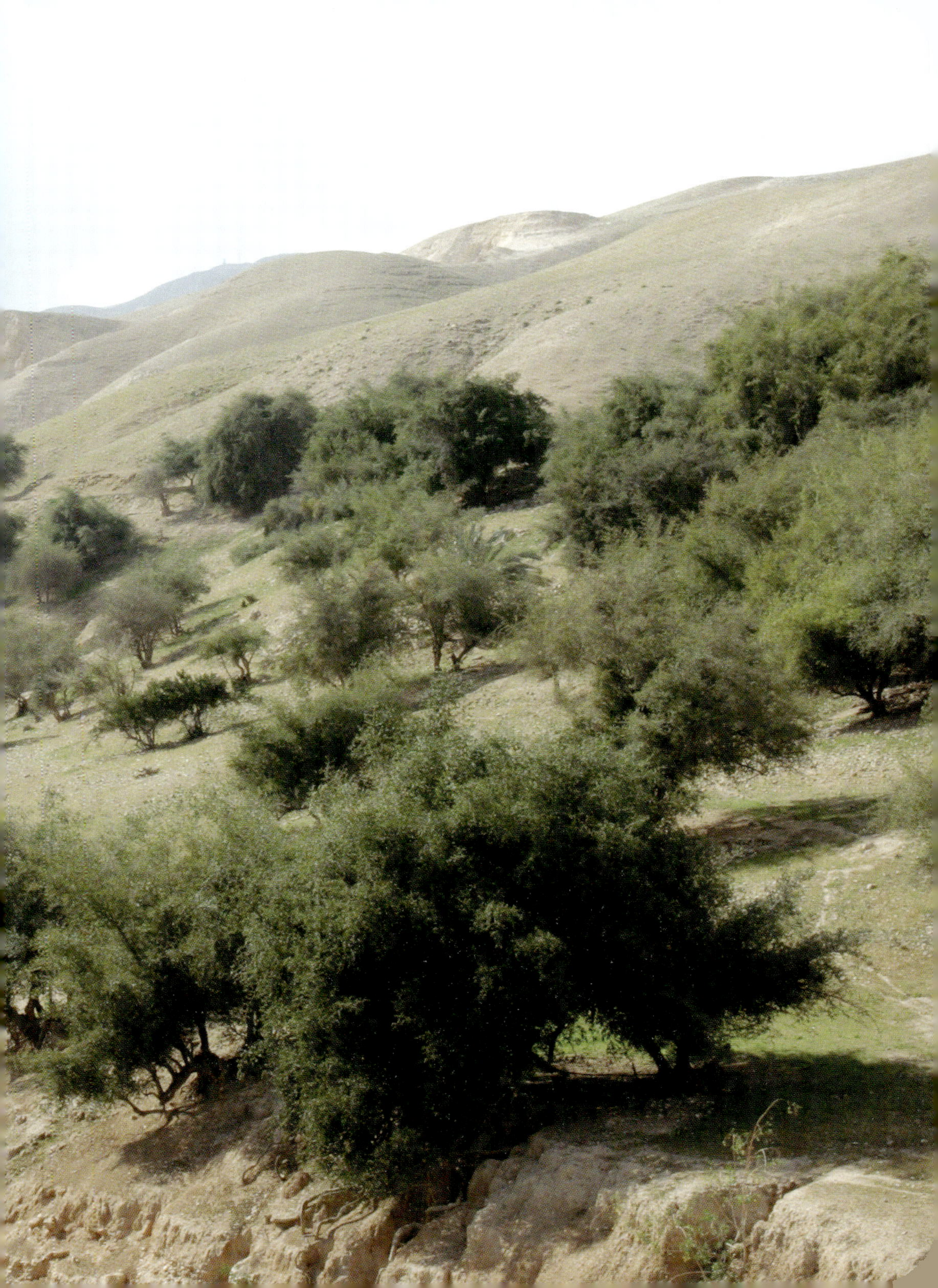

BEAUTIFUL PALESTINE *Majdi Hadid*

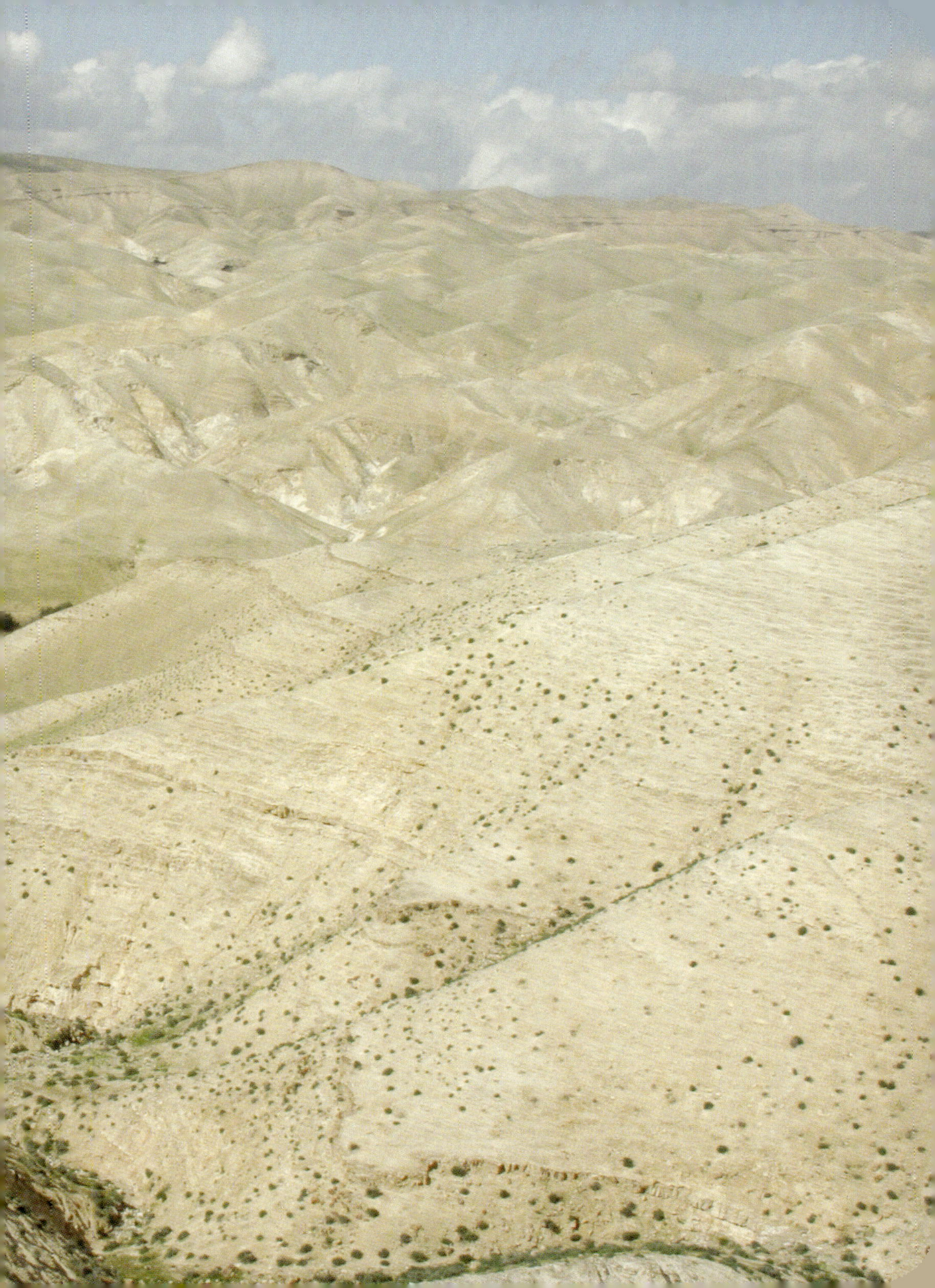

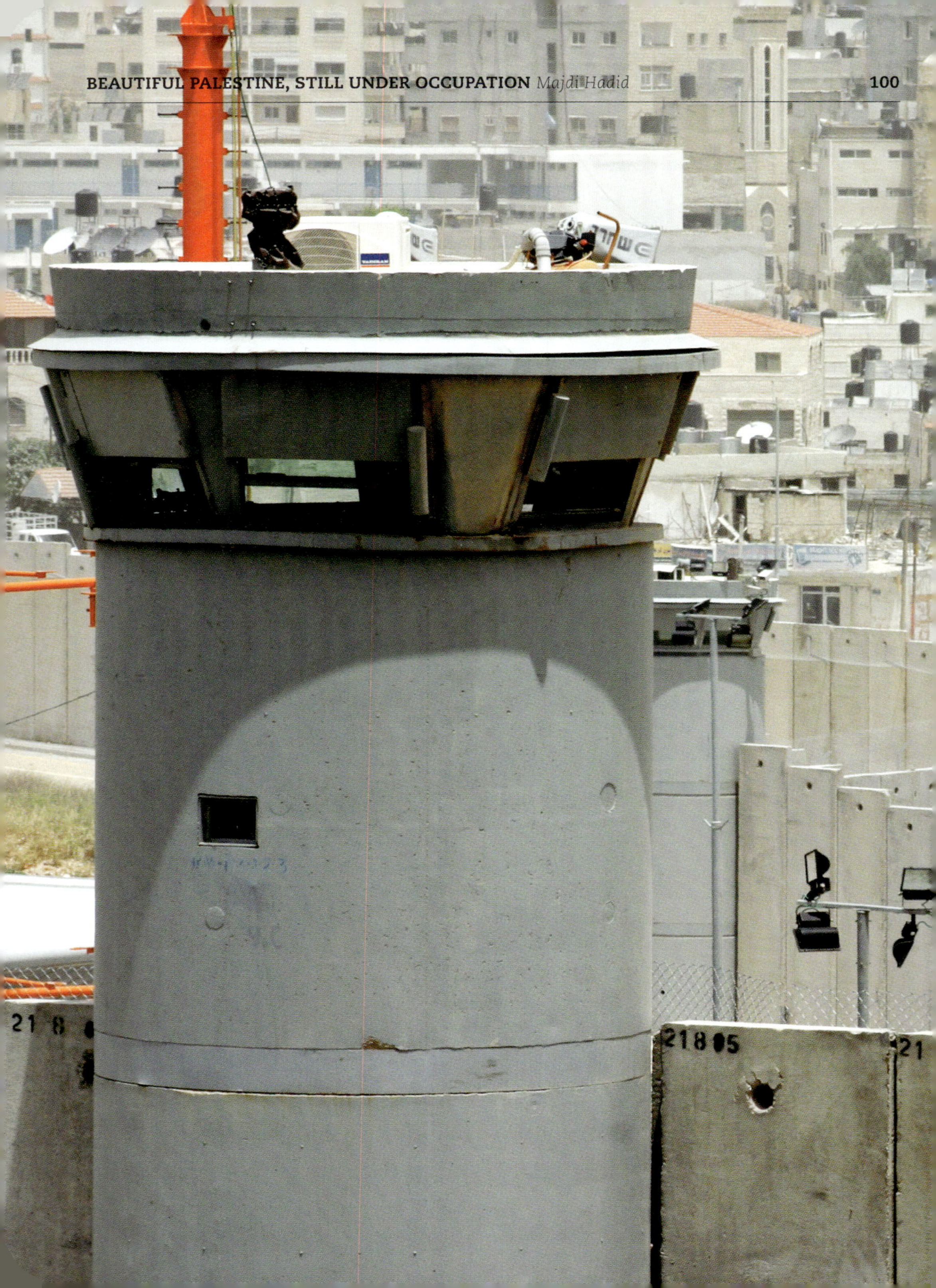
21805
21

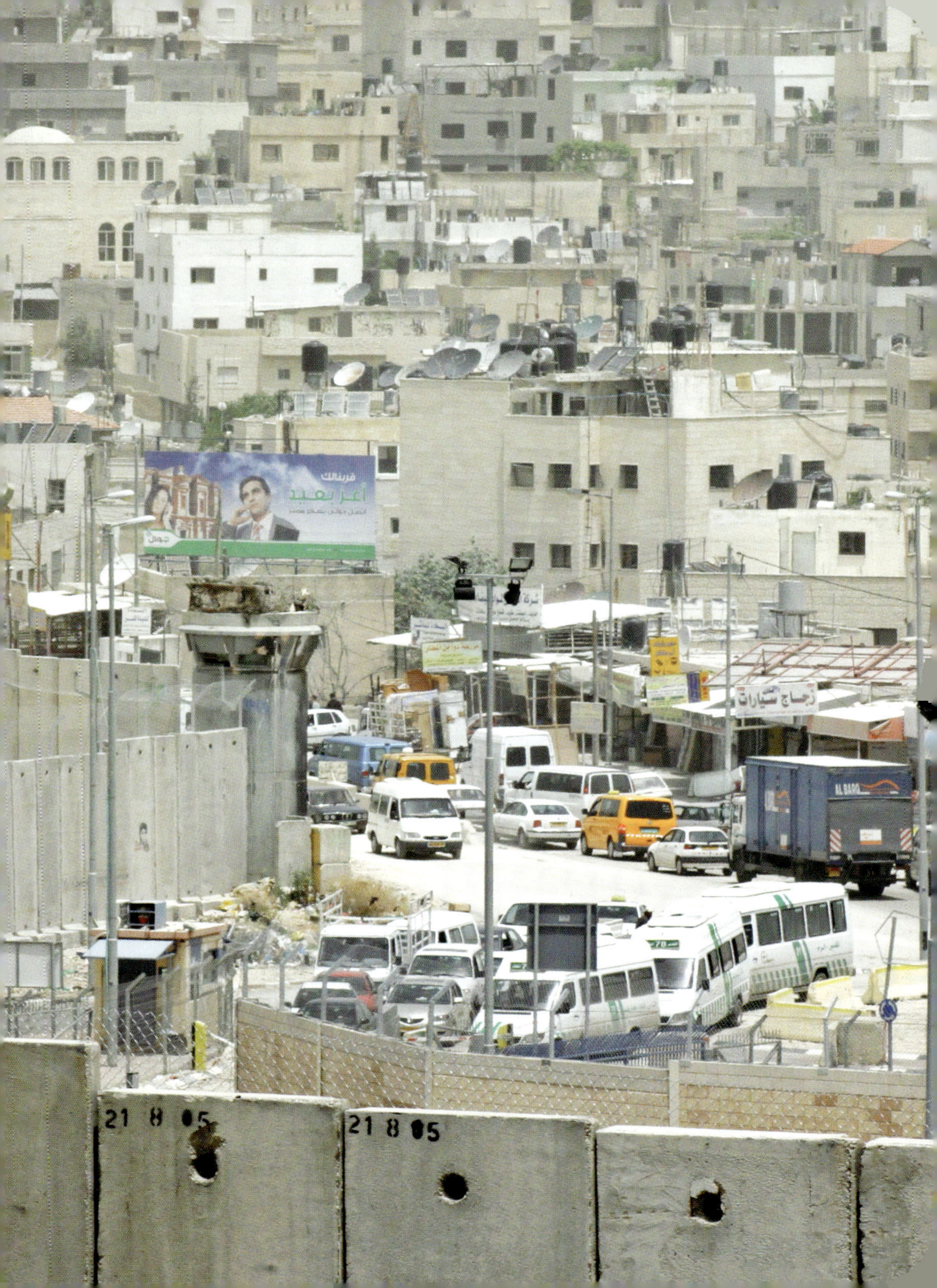

زجاج سيارات
AL BARQ
21 8 05
21 8 05

ARCHITECTURAL POSSIBILITIES FOR THE WALL *Senan Abdelqader Architects (S.A., I.M.)* 102

Green and beautiful

Connected in any way

We'll use their wall for our needs

ARCHITECTURAL POSSIBILITIES FOR THE WALL *Senan Abdelqader Architects (S.A., I.M.)* 103

Some colour would help as well

Palestinian way to the other side

Determination is what we need

FRAGMENTATION OF THE WALL *Senan Abdelqader Architects (Senan Abdelqader, Inas Moussa)* 104

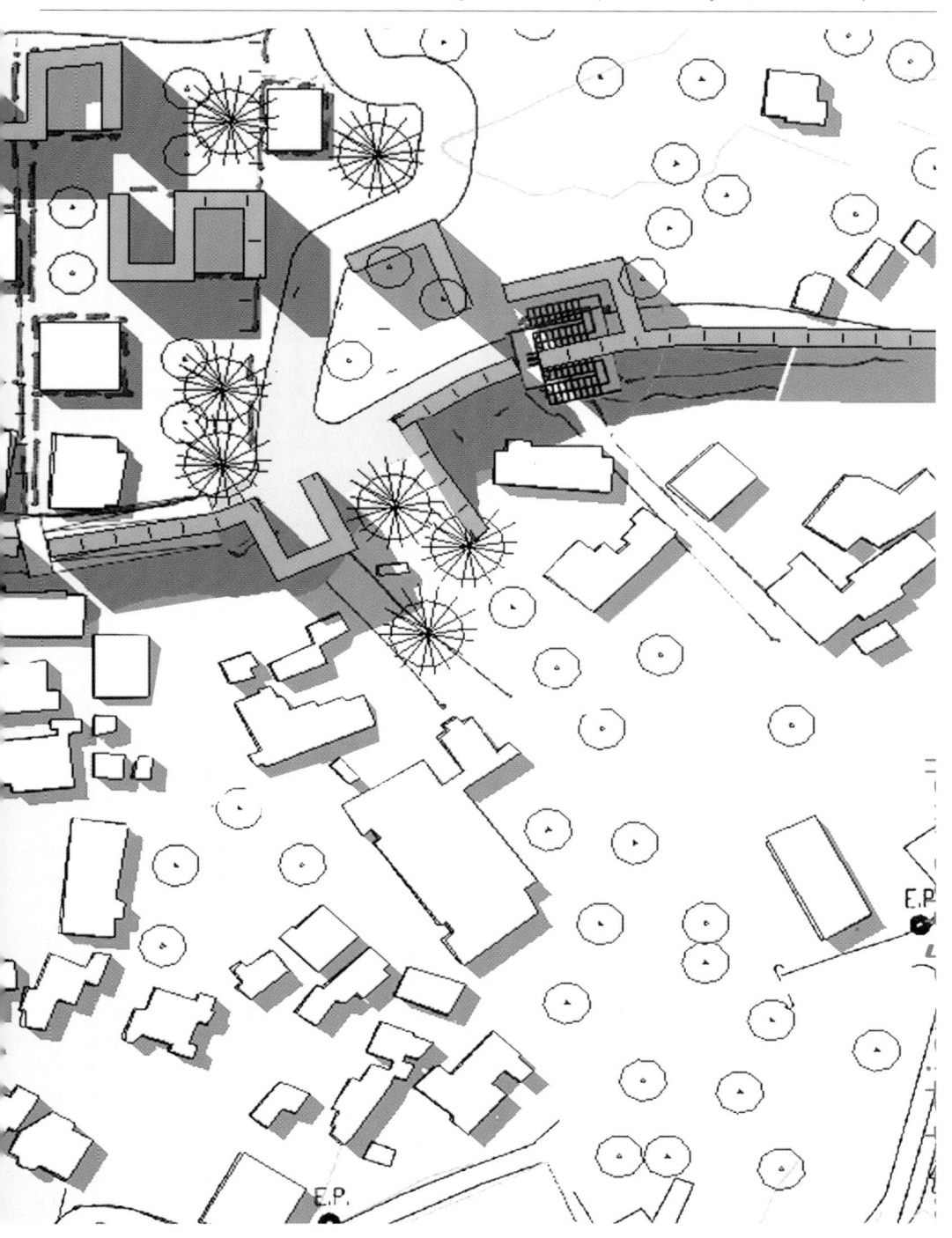

FRAGMENTATION OF THE WALL *Senan Abdelqader Architects (Senan Abdelqader, Inas Moussa)* **105**

THE EXTREMITIES OF RAMALLAH *Majd Abdel Hamid*

THE EXTREMITIES OF RAMALLAH *Majd Abdel Hamid*

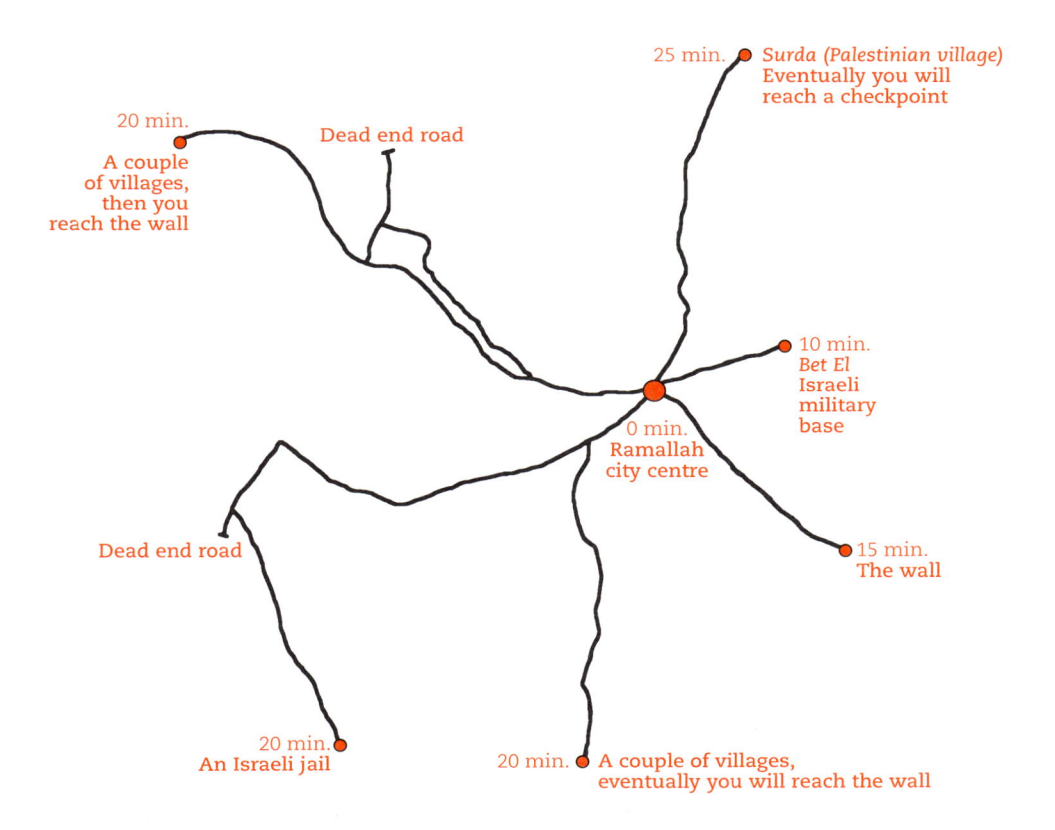

25 min. Surda (Palestinian village) Eventually you will reach a checkpoint

20 min. A couple of villages, then you reach the wall

Dead end road

10 min. Bet El Israeli military base

0 min. Ramallah city centre

Dead end road

15 min. The wall

20 min. An Israeli jail

20 min. A couple of villages, eventually you will reach the wall

SIGNS FOR WHAT'S USUALLY PROHIBITED, BUT NOT IN PALESTINE *Sami Shana'ah*

1.
Smoking allowed everywhere and at anytime

2.
Park wherever you like
No parking fees, no fines

3.
Use of mobile phones is always permitted, also during meetings

4.
Memorial

5.
Open fire

6.
Explosions

7.
Bombs

NEW ROAD SIGNS FOR PALESTINE *Maissoon Sharkawi*

1. Wall

2. Arafat

3. Please go back and try again later

4. Why are you astonished?

5. Watch out: army is nearby

6. Caution

7. Army

8. Target

9. Random indication

AT THE CHECKPOINT *Khaled Jarrar*

AT THE CHECKPOINT *Khaled Jarrar*

I live and work in Ramallah. But I used to visit my parents in the West Bank town of Jenin, some 70 miles north of Ramallah, and endure the humiliation and degradation at the checkpoints along the trip. But after Israel imposed further travel restrictions, I cut down on my visits. If it were only me, then I would have endured the hardship but my wife and two-year-old son could not take the brunt of it.

This hard situation inspired me to document such behaviours and to portray in hard evidence the extent of suffering and the predicament of ordinary Palestinians at the military checkpoints, estimated to be around 400.

My exhibition is a message to all nations and to Israelis, that what is being done at military checkpoints is in contravention of all ethics and norms and the embodiment of a racist policy against Palestinians.

The day the exhibition was to take place, I was supposed to meet Liza and Mazen who would accompany me to the Hawara checkpoint near Nablus at 8.30 am at Al-Manara in Ramallah. But I arrived one hour early and enjoyed watching the merchants on the street. The coffee seller served his first customers hot Arabic coffee; the newspaper seller told passers-by the news of the day. The taxi dropped us off just before the Hawara checkpoint, which we had to cross by foot. The photos were stored in two very heavy boxes that we had to carry a few hundred metres as we looked for the perfect spot for the exhibition. We chose a fence next to the path that those who want to cross the checkpoint from either side have to use.

I thought it was important that as many people as possible would be able to see the pictures without making an effort. This is especially important to mention because the Hawara checkpoint is one of the most difficult in the West Bank. It takes sometimes four to five hours to pass it, if at all. More than once people are sent back, without any reason.

After three hours, I closed the exhibition to go back to Ramallah. The soldiers didn't let us go without having a look at the pictures. One of the soldiers, a young woman, suddenly felt she needed to defend herself and her comrades by saying they have to protect their country and that it is legitimate to fight terrorists.

This was my first exhibition and I felt that it succeeded not only in attracting a lot of people but also in spreading the idea of fighting the occupation with art.

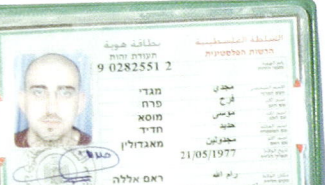

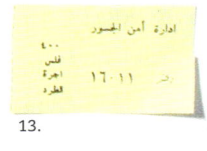

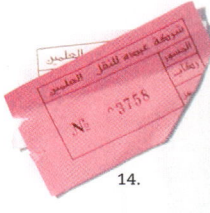

DOCUMENTS THAT I NEEDED TO TRAVEL OUTSIDE PALESTINE *Majdi Hadid*

DOCUMENTS THAT I NEEDED TO TRAVEL OUTSIDE PALESTINE *Majdi Hadid*

1. **Palestinian Passport**
   valid for three years
2. **Canadian Passport**
   valid for five years
3. **Jordanian Passport**
   Expired since 1996, almost all Palestinians have one like this, the number starts with 'T' for temporary
4. **Palestinian Identification Card**
   You cannot leave your house without it. The green colour for Palestinian and the blue ID for the Israelis
5. **'Magnetic Card'**
   another ID but this one is issued by the Israeli authorities. It facilitates transportation around the country and will allow you to apply for special permission to travel through Israel
6. **Tax Paper to cross the Israeli border 'Allenby Bridge'** 126 NIS – *New Israeli Shekels (c. € 24,–)*. It's the only way out for all the people in the West Bank
7. **The green card**
   Only for the Jordanian side. They write the entry and departure dates in and out of Jordan
8. **Bus ticket for one person from Allenby Bridge to Jericho** 12 NIS *(c. €2,–)*
9. **Single luggage ticket from Jericho to the Allenby Bridge** 2 NIS *(c. € 0,50)*
10. **Bus ticket for one person from Jericho to the Allenby Bridge** 12 NIS *(c. €2,–)*
11. **Ticket to enter the rest area in Jericho**
    There you take a bus to *Al Alami checkpoint* and then you transfer to another bus in front of the Israeli soldiers
12. **Tax paper for the Jordanian border**
    10 JD – *Jordanian Dinar (c. €11,–)*
    When you pay it you sign the other side, not to stay in Jordan for more than 30 days, otherwise you have to contact the local government office
13. **Ticket for leaving Jordanian bridge**
    400 fils *(c. € 0,50)*
14. **Two tickets** 8 NIS *(c. € 1,50)*
    Obtained from no man's land in the middle of the two bridges, where you collect your luggage to go to the Jordanian side
15. **Special permission** 70 NIS *(c. € 14,–)*
    Sold in case you don't have a valid Palestinian Passport, or if your Passport has been issued for less than 30 days from your travelling date; that's how long it takes to register the passport from the Palestinian Authority to the Israeli side
16. **Round trip ticket Amman-Jordan to Frankfurt Germany** *(c. € 500,–)*
17. **Luggage tag** from Amman to Jordan
18. **Boarding Pass** from Amman to Frankfurt
19. **Boarding Pass** from Frankfurt to Amman

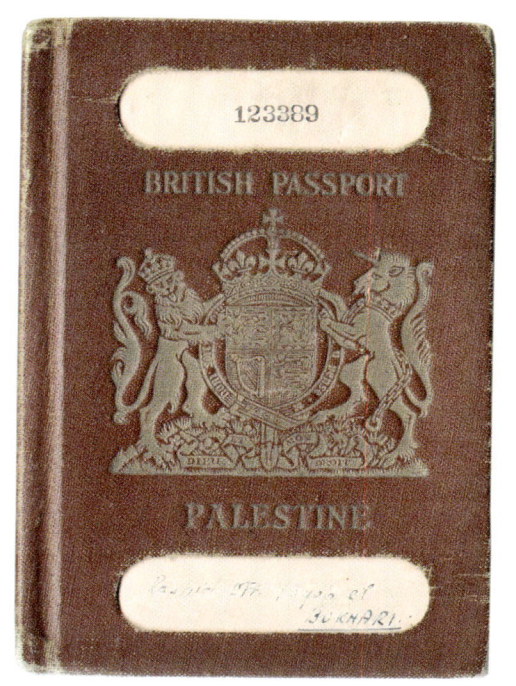

MY FATHER'S PALESTINIAN NATIONALITY *Baha Boukhary*

British Passport of Palestine, of my father Rashid EFF. Yacub Bukhari (1913), architect

"By His Majesty's High Commissioner for Palestine.

These are to request and require in the Name of His Majesty all those who it may concern to allow the bearer to pass freely without let or hindrance and to afford him every assistance and protection of which he may stand in need.

Given at Jerusalem the 10th day of August 1939."

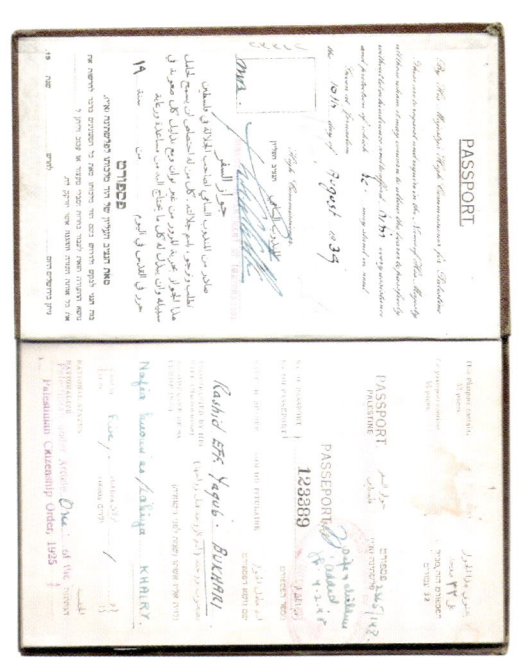

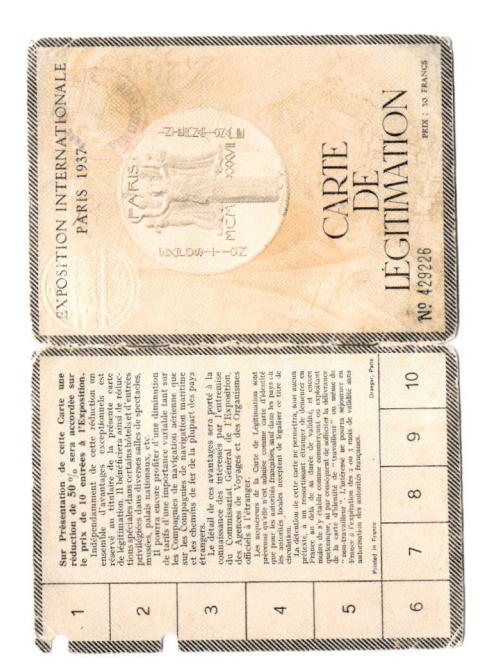

MY FATHER'S PALESTINIAN NATIONALITY *Baha Boukhary*

Identity Card International Exhibition, Paris 1937

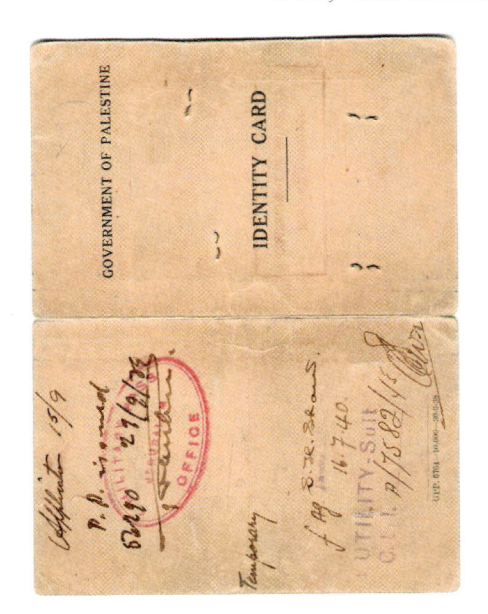

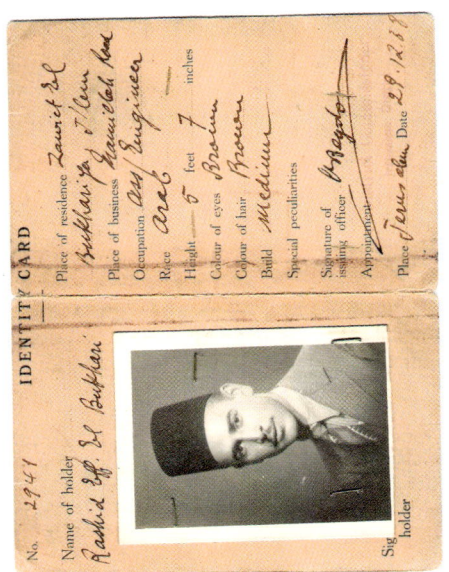

Government of Palestine, Identity Card, 1938

MY OWN HOUSE WHERE I CANNOT BE *Baha Boukari*

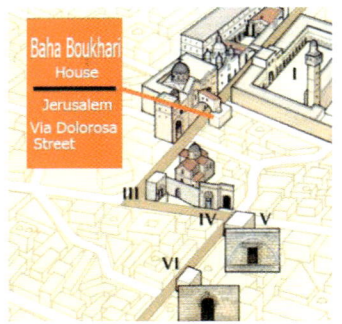

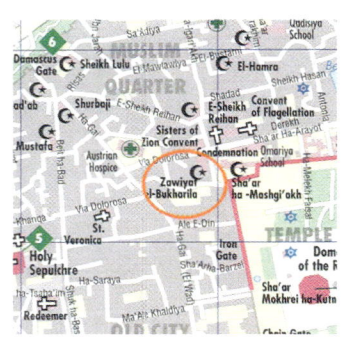

I am probably the only Palestinian whose house is drawn and mentioned on tourist maps.

Drawing by Spanish Artist, c. 1800

Photograph, 1845

Drawing by David Roberts

Postcard, Jerusalem

Me and my brother and sisters, in front of the house, 1948

House and arch

MY OWN HOUSE WHERE I CANNOT BE *Baha Bcukari*

My own painting of the house

Me in front of my house

My house in Jerusalem on the Via Dolorosa street has been in my family for generations. The house and the arch beside it were once part of a big palace and belonged to Pilatos from Rome. It is the first place to visit on a Christian Pilgrims map. There is also a mosque inside the house which is open to the public and a church which is connected to our house by the arch. We used to live in harmony and even though I was a Muslim, I was also raised in this church when I was a child.

My family history resembles the Palestinian way of life. We are open minded ordinary people who love life and want to do something with ourselves in a civilized way. Islam never stopped me from being an artist and it never stopped my father from being an architect and a pilot. He left Jerusalem in 1948 to work as an architect in Damascus when I was four years old. When we came back, the political situation had changed, and all of a sudden we were called 'immigrants'.

Now I can't live in, nor visit my house as I am not allowed to go into Jerusalem with my green ID card. The only time I can be there is when the Israelis give me permission to enter Jerusalem, for instance when I have to attend a funeral of a family member. At the moment my cousin occupies the house as he has an ID card from Jerusalem.

59 YEARS OF OCCUPATION *Basel Al Maqousi*

I am from a small village called Demra. My grandfathers left it for fear of war and death. Now this village is the point of the entrance to the occupied territories from Palestine. The time before the year 1948 was very different and can't be compared with nowadays. Palestinian people (Muslims, Jews and Christians) lived together as neighbours and friends in the historical Palestine. They worked together, shared happiness and sadness. Most of the community were peasants living in villages in small communities. They had never thought that life would be turned upside down, never dreamt that they would be separated and some of them would be enemies of each other.

In 1948, hundreds of thousands of Palestinian people ran away from the war. They left their houses to be safe somewhere else. "The war will finish soon, we will return to our houses," is what all of them believed. None of them thought that it would be Diaspora. None of them could imagine that he wouldn't be able to

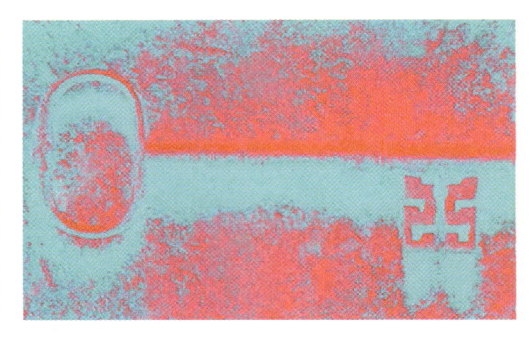

59 YEARS OF OCCUPATION *Basel Al Maqousi*

get back to his house, his trees, his horse that he left in his stable. None of them thought that he wouldn't eat again from the olives, oil, beans and grain that he'd stored for the next season. "We're just out for a few days only, until the war finishes and we're able to return." They thought that war couldn't continue forever, so when they left their houses they only took food for a few days with them, and some clothes for the children who might not be able to keep their clothes clean until they returned. People closed their door, took the key and left. Packed as if they'd gone to the market or to a visit out of the village to attend a wedding or to celebrate the harvest season.

More than 400 villages were destroyed afterwards. Thousands of houses were erased from the surface of the land. Millions of trees were plucked out. Thousands and thousands of Palestinians still keep the key of their home to return. Too many of them died carrying the key dreaming of their return.

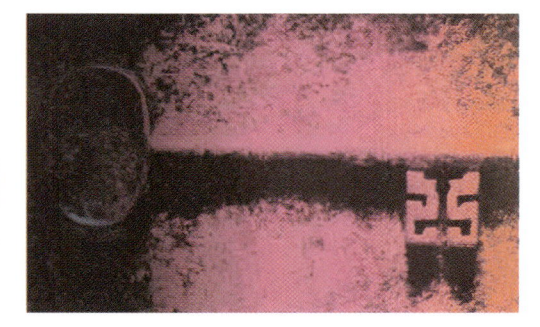

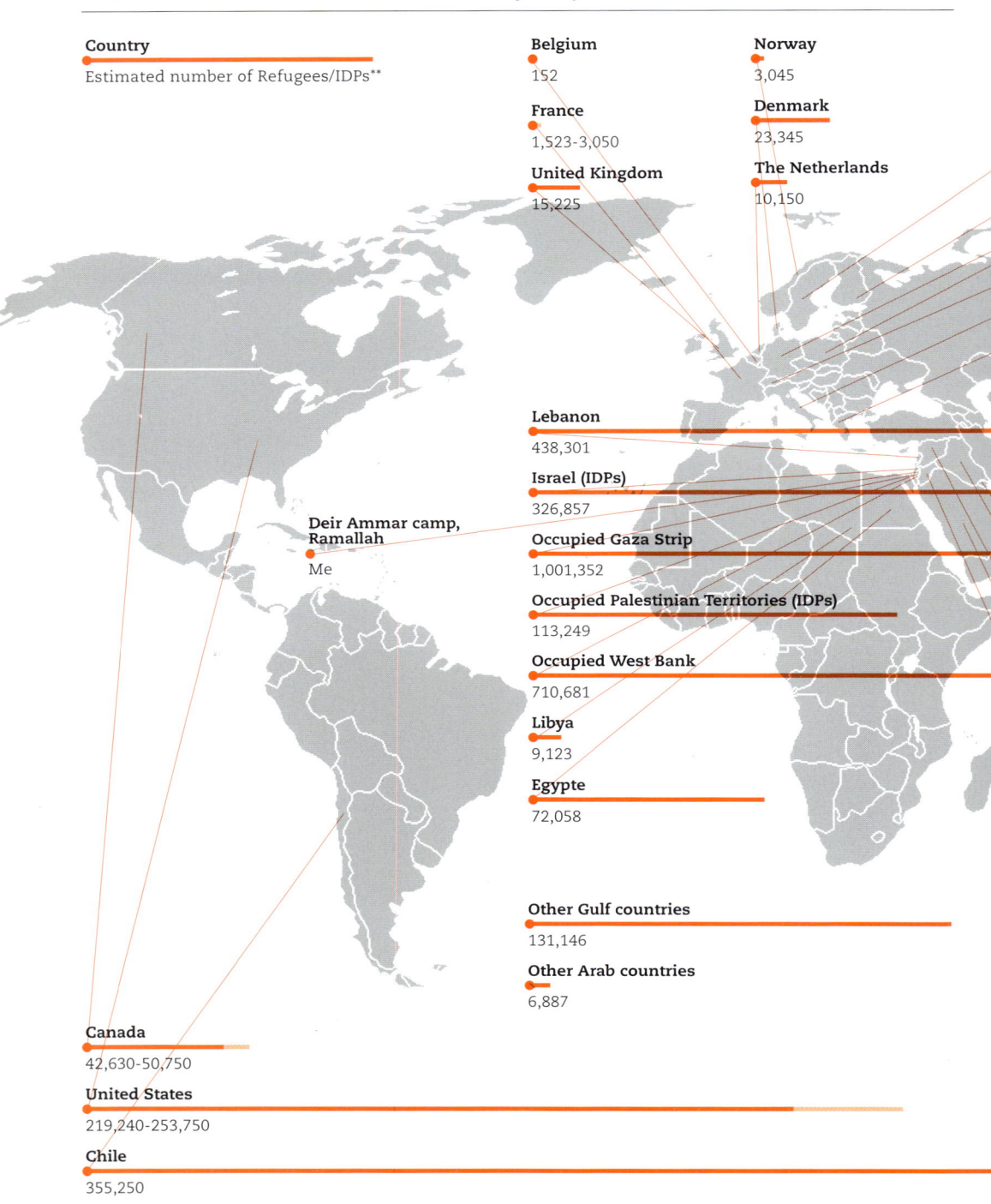

PALESTINIAN REFUGEES IN THE WORLD* *Awatef Rumiyah*

Country
Estimated number of Refugees/IDPs**

Belgium
152

France
1,523-3,050

United Kingdom
15,225

Norway
3,045

Denmark
23,345

The Netherlands
10,150

Lebanon
438,301

Israel (IDPs)
326,857

Deir Ammar camp, Ramallah
Me

Occupied Gaza Strip
1,001,352

Occupied Palestinian Territories (IDPs)
113,249

Occupied West Bank
710,681

Libya
9,123

Egypte
72,058

Other Gulf countries
131,146

Other Arab countries
6,887

Canada
42,630-50,750

United States
219,240-253,750

Chile
355,250

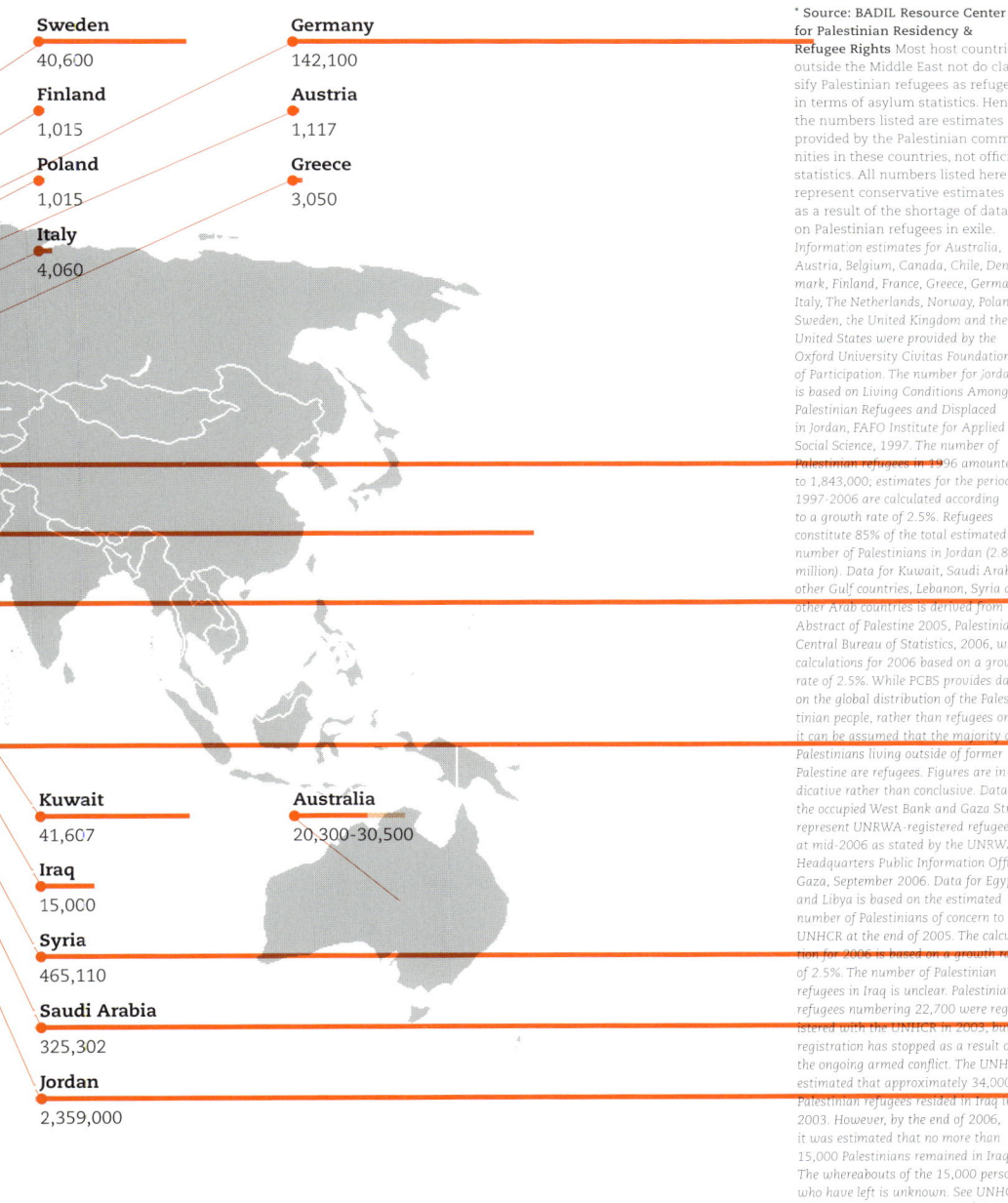

PALESTINIAN REFUGEES IN THE WORLD* *Awatef Rumiyah*

Sweden
40,600

Finland
1,015

Poland
1,015

Italy
4,060

Germany
142,100

Austria
1,117

Greece
3,050

Kuwait
41,607

Iraq
15,000

Syria
465,110

Saudi Arabia
325,302

Jordan
2,359,000

Australia
20,300-30,500

* Source: BADIL Resource Center for Palestinian Residency & Refugee Rights Most host countries outside the Middle East not do classify Palestinian refugees as refugees in terms of asylum statistics. Hence, the numbers listed are estimates provided by the Palestinian communities in these countries, not official statistics. All numbers listed here represent conservative estimates as a result of the shortage of data on Palestinian refugees in exile. Information estimates for Australia, Austria, Belgium, Canada, Chile, Denmark, Finland, France, Greece, Germany, Italy, The Netherlands, Norway, Poland, Sweden, the United Kingdom and the United States were provided by the Oxford University Civitas Foundations of Participation. The number for Jordan is based on Living Conditions Among Palestinian Refugees and Displaced in Jordan, FAFO Institute for Applied Social Science, 1997. The number of Palestinian refugees in 1996 amounted to 1,843,000; estimates for the period 1997-2006 are calculated according to a growth rate of 2.5%. Refugees constitute 85% of the total estimated number of Palestinians in Jordan (2.8 million). Data for Kuwait, Saudi Arabia, other Gulf countries, Lebanon, Syria and other Arab countries is derived from Abstract of Palestine 2005, Palestinian Central Bureau of Statistics, 2006, with calculations for 2006 based on a growth rate of 2.5%. While PCBS provides data on the global distribution of the Palestinian people, rather than refugees only, it can be assumed that the majority of Palestinians living outside of former Palestine are refugees. Figures are indicative rather than conclusive. Data for the occupied West Bank and Gaza Strip represent UNRWA-registered refugees at mid-2006 as stated by the UNRWA Headquarters Public Information Office, Gaza, September 2006. Data for Egypt and Libya is based on the estimated number of Palestinians of concern to the UNHCR at the end of 2005. The calculation for 2006 is based on a growth rate of 2.5%. The number of Palestinian refugees in Iraq is unclear. Palestinian refugees numbering 22,700 were registered with the UNHCR in 2003, but registration has stopped as a result of the ongoing armed conflict. The UNHCR estimated that approximately 34,000 Palestinian refugees resided in Iraq in 2003. However, by the end of 2006, it was estimated that no more than 15,000 Palestinians remained in Iraq. The whereabouts of the 15,000 persons who have left is unknown. See UNHCR, Aide-Memoire: Protecting Palestinians in Iraq and Seeking Humanitarian Solutions for Those Who Fled the Country, Geneva, December 2006.

** IDPs = Internally Displaced Palestinians

Ansar Prison, Negev Desert

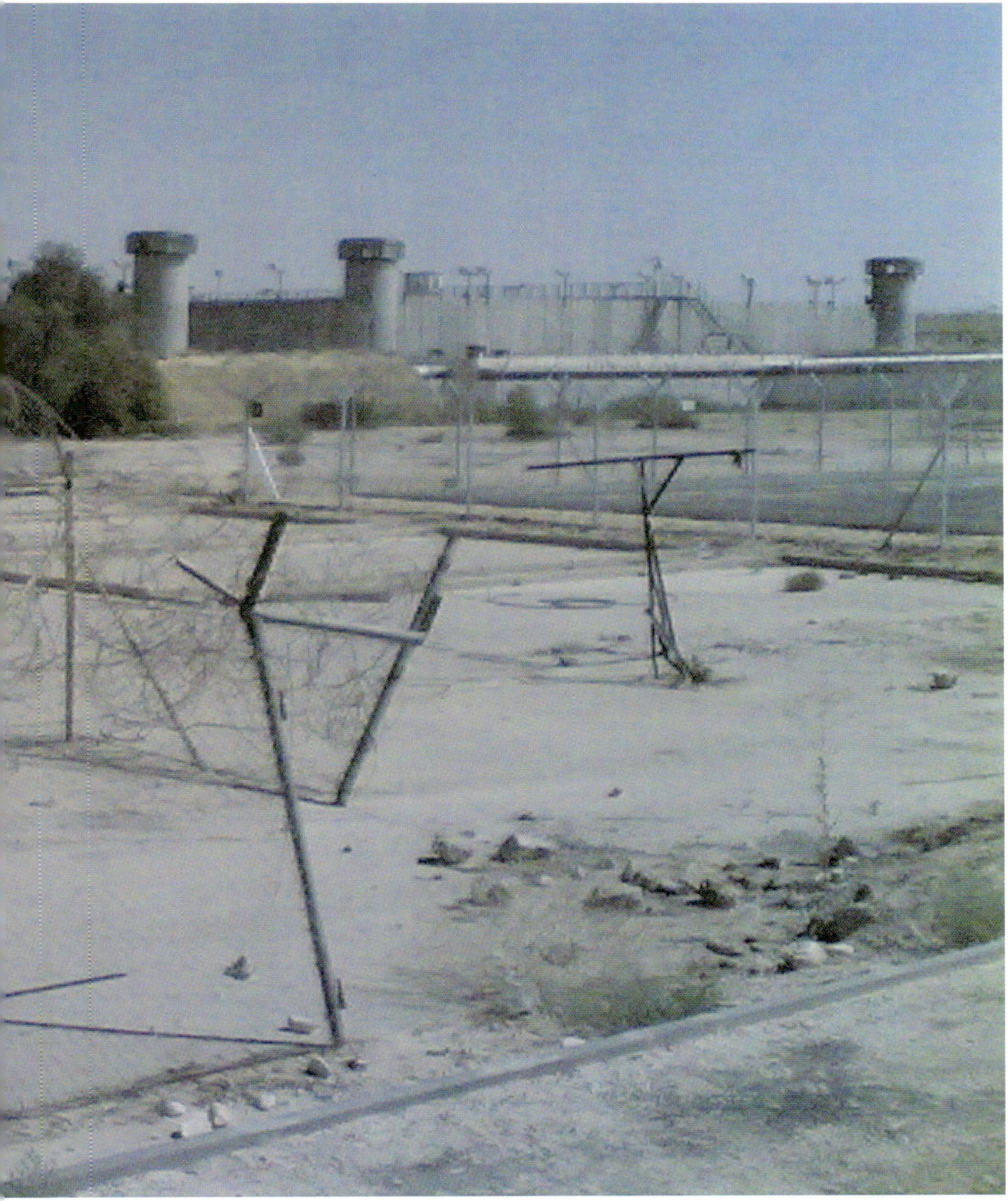

A LIFELINE TO MY BROTHER *Abed Al Jubeh*

Morning rush hour

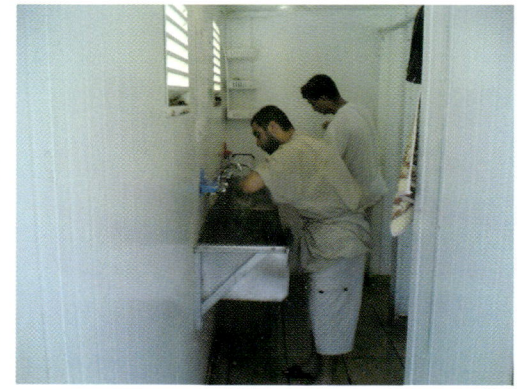

Wash hour

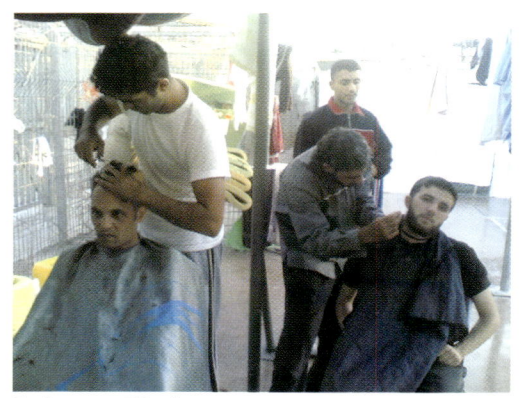

Do-it-yourself barbers

Going to the gym

Laundry day

Express airmail service

A LIFELINE TO MY BROTHER *Abed Al Jubeh*

Shopkeeping

Arts and crafts

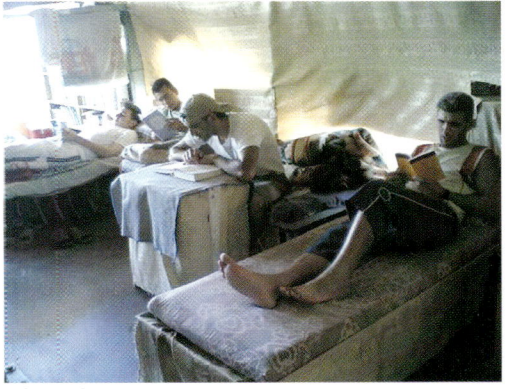

Lifelong learning

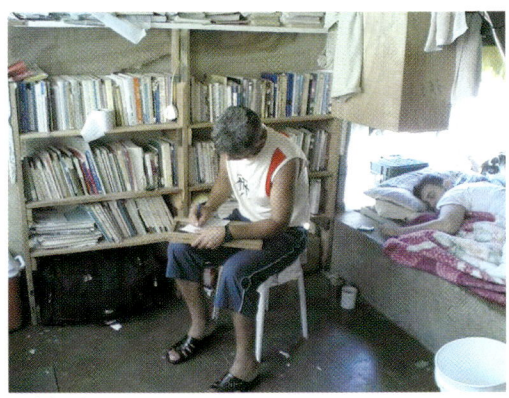

Writing home

Going to the movies

Keeping up with the outside world

A LIFELINE TO MY BROTHER *Abed Al Jubeh*

Al fresco dining

Washing up duty

A time to play

A time to pray

Between friends

Still life

A LIFELINE TO MY BROTHER *Abed Al Jubeh*

If you ask my mother to draw a map of Palestine and describe the places she's been, it always starts and ends with her prison visit to sons and brothers. There was a time when it was a full time job, visiting prisons from the Al Karmel mountains in the North to the desert of the Negev, from Askelan on the coast to Bisan in the Jordan valley. From East to West her relationship with the geography of this land is carved in the sentences of her loved ones. Today she is too tired. Not old but simply aged. Her health can no longer manage the distances and searing heat to visit her son, in the Negev desert.

 For her and us, these photos are a lifeline. They were smuggled out through mobile phone technology. Although the quality of the images is not so good, they are incredibly dear to us. They allow my daughters to see their uncle's everyday life. In these images they can see his passion for reading and literature. In every prison where he is detained, he establishes a book club, contrary to what the prison authorities want. For this reason he gets moved around a lot. We often have months of not even knowing which prison he is in and whether visits are allowed.

 On my last visit I met a family coming from Tulkarem in the North. They needed to leave home at three in the morning to see their son. Since none of the visitors is allowed to leave the prison compound until all visits are over, it took this family almost 24 hours travelling in gruelling heat to have just 45 minutes behind reinforced glass.

In Palestine, there is hardly a family who has not been affected by detention, sometimes without trial; men and women, girls and boys, of every political persuasion, class and religion. This reality is part of our landscape and the typography of our lives.

 These photos were taken by political prisoners detained in Ansar, a desert prison in a remote part of the southern Negev desert. The prison was re-opened in the first Intifada in 1987. The main photo shows the original barbed wire sections that used to separate the tents. In the background is the new prison. Although it has external walls, it is still a desert tent camp, divided into sections. At this moment there are approximately 2,700 prisoners detained in Ansar's tents. Their average age is only 20, with some detainees much younger.

LETTER FROM PRISONER MOHAMMED *Tayseer Barakat*

أهلي الأعزاء السلام عليكم
أنا بخير. لا تقلقوا علي فقفت قليلاً من السجن لكن صحتي جيدة. السجن عالم آخر
أنا اشتاق اليكم كثير بمعرفة كم هو صعب علينا أن نصبر عن الزيارات.
نحن نحاول تحسين شروط اللقاء معكم شما خلال حتى يسمحوا لنا لمس ايديكم
عبر الشباك. يا ما بدي احكيلك هالخلة ست أوعك تقولي لأبي انا
انا صادفت صرصورين قبل ٧ أيام أنا لعبا معهم وأقضي وقتي من القراءة ومراقبة
الصرصورين. وحضرت لهما علبه صغيرة وكل يوم بطعمهم رشة سكر.
واحد لونه أسود وواحد لونه بني. لكن أحوزهم عني ما بكبرا ان
وكل يوم بطلعهم من العلبة عدة ساعات
سلامي للجميع يا ما

ابنك محمد

LETTER FROM PRISONER MOHAMMED *Tayseer Barakat*

My dear parents, peace be upon you,

I am well. Do not worry about me. I have lost a little weight in prison, but I am in good health. The prison is another world. I miss you a lot and I know how hard it is to hold a strike against visitations. We are working towards better conditions for visitations; we will make great efforts to be allowed to touch your fingers through the windows.

Mom, I want to tell you something but please do not say that your son has gone crazy. Seven days ago, I befriended two cockroaches. I play with them and spend my time in between reading or watching them. I have kept them in a small box and everyday I feed them a pinch of sugar. One is black and the other is brown. I might wed them when they grow up. I let them out of the box a few hours every day.

My greetings to all, Mom
Your son Mohammed

By: Prisoner Mohammed to his family in Al-Khalil, Majido Prison 20th April

LETTER FROM PRISONER AHMAD *Tayseer Barakat*

مع خطوات الشجاعة في ردهة السجن، تتكاثر بعض ظل جيشي أبيض مثل الأمل و أصابعي تعبر من خلال الجدران (!) الأزل. وحلمي يسيل مابين أصابعي القمر الذي أراه من النافذة ليس بالقمر الذي ترونه وإنما كأنه نفسه هذا القمر هو حبّة قرص منه دواء لصداع الليل...

أهلي اني رأيت أركب خيول الخيـلاء وتأتيكم افتحوا الباب الآن. قلبي نجمة كسمكة قديمة من الحكمة والبكاء

أنا القمر الذي ضاع اسما واسمي مكتوب بالأرقام

مع جثتي التي تملأ الكأس ثملاً

With the sounds of the footsteps of the prison guard in the corridor of the prison, my pulse races like a white army, like hope, and my fingers penetrate the walls to eternity, and my dream spills through my fingers.

The moon I see through the window is not the moon you see, even if it is the circular tablet, the painkiller of the night headaches...

My family, now I ride on the shuttle of imagination and I come to you. Open the door now, seeing that my heart is aching from wisdom and tears, like an old fish.

I am the number that has become a name.
And a name written with numbers.

With my love that fills the glass with sun.

Ahmad

By: Prisoner Ahmad Yousef, Gaza, Beir Sabe' Prison, 1997

LETTER FROM PRISONER ALI *Tayseer Barakat*

أمي الحبيبة كيف حال والدي
إتعلمت الكتابة وكتبتلك يمه
السلام عليكي

إبنك علي - حكيم عسقل

LETTER FROM PRISONER ALI *Tayseer Barakat*

My beloved mother how are you and my father

I learned to read and write mother

Greetings to all
Your son Ali
(Asqalan prison)

By: Prisoner Ali from Nablus to his mother, Asqalan Prison, 2001

بسم الله الرحمن الرحيم

زوجي العزيز المحترم أبو صلاح – بأهدي إليك كل الإحترام والوفاء وولاء خالص وآخر القبلات إليك ... تعبت من بعدك يا أبو صلاح وبتني سوف أتحمل أكثر وأكثر لأنني بحبك وسأظل أصبك وأصلصلك وأوفي لك بعهدك و أهلك وأشهد الله إن ظلت على قيد الحياة أن أبقى مخلصه وفيه لك مهما طال أسرك قبل أن يعتقلوك كان وزني ٧٠ كيلو أما الآن أصبحت ٥٠ كيلو صرت مثل الطفل الصغير . لا أكل كل الأكلات إلي كنت تحبها فالحياة والأكل له طعم لغيابك عنك .

بنحب . بخبرك محمد بخير وخاصه الأولاد . ودايماً بيسألون ويقولون وين أبوكي وخاصه أبو العلم مرات يقول لا بو بلال يا بابا .

دير بالك على حالك يا أبو صلاح بستنى يوم اللقاء لو ما ظل من العمر أيام

زوجتك عابده

LETTER TO PRISONER ABU SALAH *Tayseer Barakat*

In the name of God
My dear and respected husband Abu Salah,

I send you all respect, devotion and warm kisses... Your absence has tired me Abu Salah, but I will endure more and more because I love you I will carry on loving you and being devoted and loyal to you as long as I live. I give you my word, and for as long as I shall live, that I will be faithful to you regardless of the length of your imprisonment. Before they arrested you I weighed 70kg but now I weigh 50kg, just like a little child. I do not eat your favourite meals, for food is tasteless without you.

I would like to tell you that we are all well, especially the children. They always think about you and they constantly ask where is dad, especially Abu El-Soloh, and sometimes he even calls Abu Bilal, dad. Take care Abu Salah.

I am waiting to be united with you one day, even if there were no days left in my life.

Your wife Aida

By: Aida, a woman from Ramallah to her husband in Jnaid Prison, 2002

NO NEWS FROM PALESTINE *Khaled Hourani*

POST CARD
PALESTINE

حقوق الطبع والنشر محفوظة بمقتضى القانون

No News from Palestine
Fawanees Restaurants, Ramallah 2007

NO NEWS FROM PALESTINE *Khaled Hourani* 137

POST CARD
PALESTINE

حقوق الطبع والنشر محفوظة بمقتضى القانون

No News from Palestine
Fawanees Restaurants, Ramallah 2007

NO NEWS FROM PALESTINE *Khaled Hourani* 138

POST CARD
PALESTINE

No News from Palestine
Deer Jareer Village, Ramallah 2007

NO NEWS FROM PALESTINE *Khaled Hourani*

No News from Palestine
Deer Jareer Village, Ramallah 2007

NO NEWS FROM PALESTINE *Khaled Hourani* 140

POST CARD
PALESTINE

حقوق الطبع والنشر محفوظة بمقتضى القانون

No News from Palestine
Al Ersaal Street, Ramallah 2007

NO NEWS FROM PALESTINE *Khaled Hourani* 141

POST CARD
PALESTINE

حقوق الطبع والنشر محفوظة بمقتضى القانون

No News from Palestine
Al Ersaal Street, Ramallah 2007

NO NEWS FROM PALESTINE *Khaled Hourani* 142

POST CARD
PALESTINE

حقوق الطبع والنشر محفوظة بمقتضى القانون

No News from Palestine
From Home, Ramallah 2007

NO NEWS FROM PALESTINE *Khaled Hourani* 143

POST CARD
PALESTINE

حقوق الطبع والنشر محفوظة بمقتضى القانون

No News from Palestine
From Home, Ramallah 2007

NEW FLAGS FOR PALESTINE

Bread flag
Majd Abdel Hamid

Watermelon
Khaled Hourani

NEW FLAGS FOR PALESTINE

10 Per Cent
Munther Jaber

Parts
Majd Abdel Hamid

NEW FLAGS FOR PALESTINE

Where is the flag?
Inass Yassin

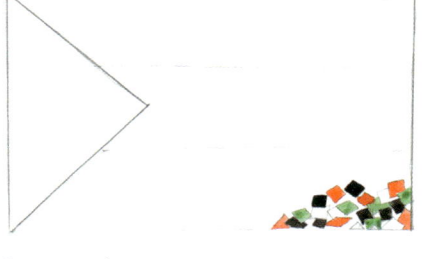

Fragmented
Hosni Radwan

Wired
Khaled Jarrar

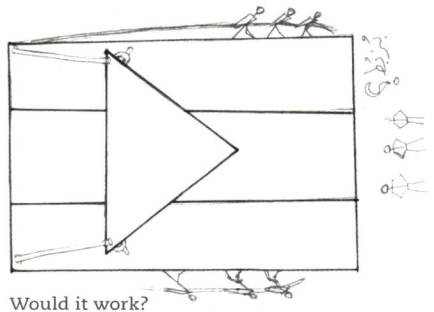

Would it work?
Inass Yassin

What did it look like?
Inass Yassin

What did it look like?
Inass Yassin

New wave
Hosni Radwan

No horizon
Hosni Radwan

NEW FLAGS FOR PALESTINE 147

Flowering flag
Majed Shala

Untitled
Basel Al Magose

Untitled
Basel Al Magose

Untitled
Basel Al Magose

Separation I
Reem Fadda

Separation II
Reem Fadda

Separation III
Reem Fadda

Separation IV
Reem Fadda

NEW FLAGS FOR PALESTINE

Siege
Awatef Rumiyah

Bullet proof
Majdi Hadid

Space
Awatef Rumiyah

Pieces
Majdi Hadid

Hurricane
Reem Fadda

Hope
Reem Fadda

Maissoon Sharbawi

Maissoon Sharbawi

NEW FLAGS FOR PALESTINE

Labyrinth
Baha Boukhari

Forward
Awatef Rumiyah

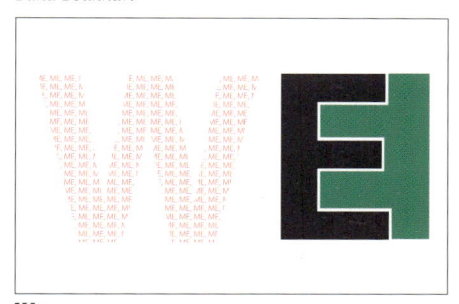

We
Hafez Omar

Key
Dima Hourani

Love
Majdi Hadid

Luck
Majdi Hadid

Maissoon Sharbawi

Maissoon Sharbawi

NEW FLAGS FOR PALESTINE

150

Moving identity I
Khaled Jarrar

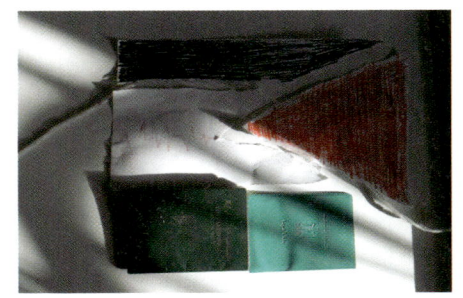

Moving identity II
Khaled Jarrar

Moving identity III
Khaled Jarrar

Moving identity IV
Khaled Jarrar

Moving identity V
Khaled Jarrar

Moving identity VI
Khaled Jarrar

Moving identity VII
Khaled Jarrar

Moving identity VIII
Khaled Jarrar

NEW FLAGS FOR PALESTINE

Living flag
Majd Abdel Hamid

INDEX OF CONTRIBUTORS

Majd Abdel Hamid
Damascus, 1988
Fine arts student

majd.hamid@gmail.com
www.artmajeur.com/majd88

Clean Ramallah, 58-59
Maps of Palestine, 19
New flags for Palestine, 144, 145, 151
The extremities of Ramallah, 106-107
The yellow cabs of Palestine, 54-55
Well informed, 40-43

Senan Abdelqader
Taibeh, 1962
Architect

senan1@zahav.net.il
www.senan-architects.com

Architectural possibilities for the wall, 102-103
Fragmentation of the wall, 104-105

Sameh Abboushi
Haifa, 1943
Artist and Architect

Maps of Palestine, 14

Tayseer Barakat
Gaza Jabalia Camp, 1959
Artist

tayseer@p-ol.com

Letter from prisoner Ahmad, 130-131
Letter from prisoner Ali, 132-133
Letter from prisoner Mohammed, 128-129
Letter to prisoner Abu Salah, 134-135
Maps of Palestine, 14

Sami Bandak
Consultant

projectsintl@googlemail.com

Maps of Palestine, 12

INDEX OF CONTRIBUTORS

Baha Boukhari
Jerusalem, 1944
Artist and cartoonist

baha@planet.com
www.baha-cartoon.net

Daily reflections on the news, 44-47
Maps of Palestine, 12
My father's Palestinian nationality, 114-115
My own house where I cannot be, 116-117
New flags for Palestine, 149

Reem Fadda
Kuwait, 1979
Academic Officer
International Academy
of Art Palestine

reemfadda@gmail.com
www.artacademy.ps

A Palestinian music collection, 36-39
Maps of Palestine, 15
New flags for Palestine, 147, 148
The flowering heritage of Palestine, 88-91
This week in Palestine, 26-27

Majdi Hadid
Ramallah, 1977
Graphic designer
and photographer

majdi@beautifulpalestine.com
www.beautifulpalestine.com

Beautiful Palestine, 92-99
Beautiful Palestine, still under occupation, 100-101
Documents that I needed to travel outside Palestine, 112-113
Maps of Palestine, 16-17
New flags for Palestine, 148, 149

Shuruq Harb
Ramallah, 1980
Artist

harbsh80@yahoo.com

Maps of Palestine, 19
In the absence of a currency, 48-51

Dima Hourani
Ramallah, 1985
Graphic designer

damdomte@hotmail.com

Maps of Palestine, 19
New flags for Palestine, 149

INDEX OF CONTRIBUTORS

Khaled Hourani
Ramallah, 1965
Director
International Academy
of Arts Palestine

khhourani@gmail.com
www.artacademy.ps

Maps of Palestine, 13
New flags for Palestine, 144
No news from Palestine, 136-143

Munther Jaber
Ramallah, 1967
Graphic designer

muntherjaber@mac.com

A user's guide to Argeelah, 62-63
Maps of Palestine, 15
New flags for Palestine, 145
Selection of Argeelah designs, 64-65

Khaled Jarrar
Jenin, 1976
Graphic designer and
freelance photographer

info@palgallery.com
www.palgallery.com

At the checkpoint, 110-111
Maps of Palestine, 18
New flags for Palestine, 146, 150
The creations of the Palestinians, 72-73
What better time than Christmas to discuss
    the positive sites of life, 68-69

Abed Al Jubeh
Jerusalem, 1965
Director Khalil Sakakini
Cultrual Centre, Ramallah

abedaljubeh@hotmail.com
www.sakakini.org

A lifeline to my brother, 122-127

Yazan Khalili
Damascus, 1981
Architect

yazan81@gmail.com
www.zanstudio.com

Colour Correction, 56-57

INDEX OF CONTRIBUTORS

Basel Al Maqousi
Gaza City, 1971
Artist

basel502@yahoo.com
www.artwfg.ps

New flags for Palestine, 147
59 years of occupation, 118-119

Suleiman Mansour
Birzeit, 1947
Artist

alwasiti@planet.com

Twelve ways to eat chickpeas, 60-61

Inas Moussa
Jerusalem, 1980
Architect

inas_moussa@yahoo.com
www.senan-architects.com

Architectural possibilities for the wall, 102-103
Fragmentation of the wall, 104-105

Hafez Omar
Tulkarem, 1983
Graphic designer

hafezomar@yahoo.com

Art School drawings after four years in Nablus, 22-23
Maps of Palestine, 18
New flags for Palestine, 149

Hosni Radwan
Bagdad, 1955
Graphic designer

hosni@p-ol.ps

Good morning Palestine, 24-25
Imagining a currency, 52-53
Maps of Palestine, 18, 19
New flags for Palestine, 146

INDEX OF CONTRIBUTORS

Awatef Rumiyah
Dier Ammar Camp, 1983
Graphic designer

iml@maktoob.com

Maps of Palestine, 18
New flags for Palestine, 148, 149
Palestinian refugees in the world, 120-121

Shareef Sarhan
Gaza, 1976
Photographer and freelance designer

shareef@artwfg.ps
www.artwfg.ps

Children in Gaza trying to play in the world's largest prison, 70-71

Sami Shana'ah
Syrai, 1980
Producer

sami@idiomsfilm.com
www.idiomsfilm.com

A normal day in the Cultural Palace, Ramallah, 35
Signs for what's usually prohibited, but not in Palestine, 108

Majed Shala
Gaza, 1960
Artist

majedart@yahoo.com
www.artwfg.ps

New flags for Palestine, 147

Maissoon Sharkawi
1978
Programmes and Activity Coordinator NGO

maissoun@gmail.com

Maps of Palestine, 18
New flags for Palestine, 148, 149
New road signs for Palestine, 109

INDEX OF CONTRIBUTORS

Mamoun Shrietch
Ramallah, 1982
Technician
International Academy
of Arts Palestine

ashreteh@yahoo.com
www.artacademy.ps

Maps of Palestine, 12
Smoke, 66-67

Lena Sobeh / RIWAQ
Russia, 1964
Graphic designer

lenasobeh@yahoo.com

Palestinian floor tiles, 74-75

Mohanad Yaqubi
Kuwait, 1981
Art director

mohanad@idiomsfilm.com
www.idiomsfilm.com

Maps of Palestine, 18
Palestinian Dress #1, 76-81
Palestinian Dress #2, 82-87

Inass Yassin
Asira, 1973
Artist and
project manager
at the virtual gallery
Birzeit University

enasmari@yahoo.com
virtualgallery.birzeit.edu

Maps of Palestine, 18
My Palestine, 20-21
New flags for Palestine, 146

This week in Palestine
Since May 1998
Editor: Sani P. Meo

sani@turbo-design.com
www.thisweekinpalestine.com

Cultural events April 2007, 28-34
This week in Palestine, 26-27

CREDITS

Subjective Atlas of Palestine
www.subjectiveatlasofpalestine.info

The *Subjective Atlas of Palestine* is an initiative of the Department for Democratisation and Peacebuilding of ICCO in the Netherlands and Dutch designer Annelys de Vet. The publication, that started with a workshop, was made possible in close collaboration with the International Academy of Arts, Palestine. In April 2007 three Dutch designers and an artist visited the Academy to work with more than two dozen Palestinian designers, artists, photographers, architects and students.

International Academy of Arts, Palestine
www.artacademy.ps

ICCO, the Netherlands
www.icco.nl

ICCO is the interchurch organization for development cooperation. It gives financial support and advice to local organizations and networks across the globe that are committed to providing access to basic social services, bringing about fair economic development and promoting peace and democracy. Moreover it brings enterprising people in the Netherlands and in developing countries into contact with each other. ICCO works in close cooperation with social organizations, including development organizations, educational organizations and the business community. For instance, it helps people in Latin America, Asia, Africa and Eastern Europe to achieve a dignified existence and economic independence. In the Middle East ICCO focuses on promoting peace and democracy, and particularly on the right of self-determination of the Palestinians. In this way, it hopes to contribute to democracy, equality and a just and sustainable peace, which offers freedom and security for all Israelis and Palestinians.

Workshop
Organizers:
Reem Fadda
Khaled Hourani
Annelys de Vet
Manon Wolfkamp (ICCO)

Guidance in Ramallah:
Rudy J. Luijters
Meike Sloover
Annelys de Vet
Samantha van der Werff

With special thanks to
Abed Al Jubeh
Khaled Hourani
Michiel Schwarz
Malkit Shoshan
Mieke Zagt

Concept & editing
Annelys de Vet

Contributors
Sameh Abboushi
Majd Abdel Hamid
Senan Abdelqader
Mohammed Amous
Tayseer Barakat
Sami Bandak
Baha Boukhari
Mahmoud Darwish (poem)
Reem Fadda
Shadi Habib Allah
Majdi Hadid
Shuruq Harb
Dima Hourani
Khaled Hourani
Munther Jaber
Khaled Jarrar
Abed Al Jubeh
Hassan Khader (foreword)
Yazan Khalili
Suleiman Mansour
Basel Al Maqousi
Sani P. Meo
Inas Moussa
Hafez Omar
Hosni Radwan
Awatef Rumiyah
Ahmad Saleem
Shareef Sarhan
Majed Shala
Sami Shana'ah
Maissoon Sharkawi
Mamoun Shrietch
Lena Sobeh
Mohanad Yaqubi
Inass Yassin

English text correction
John Kirkpatrick

Graphic design
Annelys de Vet i.c.w. all contributors

Photography
Yazan Khalili (cover)
Rudy J. Luijters et al. (portraits)

Printing
Blackprint Nyomda (Hungary),
through Meester & De Jonge (Lochem)

© 2007 The authors and 010 Publishers, Rotterdam
Permission is granted to freely use and disseminate any of the material in this book, provided that the source is correctly acknowledged and the author(s) informed.

www.010publishers.nl
ISBN 978 90 6450 648 2